Between the Lines

Sources for
Singing the Living Tradition

EDITED BY JACQUI JAMES

SECOND EDITION

BOSTON
SKINNER HOUSE BOOKS

Printed in Canada.

ISBN 1-55896-331-6
978-1-55896-331-3

10 9 8 7 6 5 4 3
09 08 07

Every effort has been made to ensure accuracy. If you have any corrections, please send them to: Editor, Unitarian Universalist Association of Congregations, 25 Beacon St., Boston, MA 02108.

Corrected reprint published in 2001.

Contents

Preface

This rich mine of personal, historical, and literary lore is designed to supplement the use of the hymnbook, *Singing the Living Tradition*. This volume also includes suggestions for improving congregational singing, a pronunciation guide, and translations for hymns and songs in languages other than English.

A new hymnbook creates special opportunities for learning. Much of the material in *Singing the Living Tradition* is familiar and easy to sing. Congregations will use it in their accustomed ways. Other songs and readings will be less familiar to many congregations. Successfully introducing and teaching new material can enrich worship for years to come. A successful introduction of new material can improve the level of congregational singing, for good singing doesn't just happen. While people love to sing, musicians and clergy must work together to develop a process to strengthen congregational singing. The section "Suggestions for Improving Congregational Singing" will help you use the material in the new hymnbook more effectively.

Special thanks to Mark Belletini, Kristen Jewett, and Helen Pickett for their help with the research for this book.

Suggestions for
Improving Congregational Singing

1. **Play the hymn/song all the way through before singing.**
   The tune may be played as a prelude, then between readings, lessons, or meditations so that the melody becomes familiar to the congregation before it begins to sing.

2. **Identify the melody line.**
   Be sure to bring out the melody while playing the hymn through. Many people do not know that the tune lies in the topmost notes, above the text. Urge people to begin noticing the contours of the melody line, to the extent of following the notes with their finger as the hymn is being announced.

3. **Support the melody line.**
   When a new hymn is being introduced, urge everyone (including the choir) who sings alto, tenor, and bass (ATB) to join with others in singing only the melody. ATB people are usually music readers and, unless otherwise requested, are apt to sing their non-melody vocal lines, thus depriving non-music readers of support as they strive to master a new melody.

4. **Lead the song.**
   Leadership means maintaining eye contact, using your strong, projecting voice, and being in charge. The leader can also indicate the contour of the music with hand motions, etc.

5. **Teach hymns and songs before the service.**
   Teach new hymns and songs to the congregation during the gathering time before worship. It only takes five to ten minutes to teach a new hymn line by line.

6. **Understand the role of the accompanist.**
   The accompanist can do more than anyone else to develop good hymn singing. If no leader is standing in front of the congregation directing with gestures, the person playing the hymns is the conductor. The accompanist can indicate from the keyboard the mood and tempo of

the music and can communicate the phrasing and some of the meaning of the text.

7. **Prepare the choir.**
   Rehearse the choir on all congregational music. The choir's primary role here is to prompt and lead the congregation. Even though hymns are generally easier than anthems, they also require rehearsal. When introducing new hymns, ask the choir members to sing just the melody. The altos, tenors, and basses can give strong leadership by singing in unison.

8. **Stop if people are confused or the song isn't working.**
   No one wants to sing poorly, so give people a chance to try again, from the beginning if necessary.

9. **Provide training and singing opportunities.**
   The presence or absence of many opportunities for singing hymns (in addition to public worship) affect congregational singing. Try a regular (perhaps monthly) hymn-sing/songfest before or after the Sunday service. You may also wish to try an evening potluck and hymn-sing.

10. **Special tips for rounds and canons.**
    Divide the group into parts.
    Tell them when to come in and how many times to sing.
    In a large room, have the parts face each other and sing to each other so that everyone can hear the round.

Notes on Hymns

1   May Nothing Evil Cross This Door
Louis Untermeyer (1885-1977), US jewelry manufacturer and vice president of Untermeyer-Robbins Co., is better known as a poet and as an editor of poetry anthologies. This poem comes from *This Singing World*, 1923.
>   OLDBRIDGE. Robert N. Quaile (b. 1867), a Methodist minister's son
>   and businessperson in Mallow, Ireland, composed this tune in 1903.
>   It was first published in *The English Hymnal*, 1906.

2   Down the Ages We Have Trod
John Andrew Storey (1935-1998) is a British Unitarian minister. A prolific poet and hymn text writer, he served on the commission that created the British Unitarian hymnbook, *Hymns for Living*, 1985. This text provides an overview of complex theological ideas in clear, accessible language.
>   WOODLAND. Thomas Benjamin (1940-), professor of music theory at
>   the Peabody Conservatory of the Johns Hopkins University, attends
>   the Unitarian Universalist Society of Howard County, Columbia,
>   Maryland. This tune was commissioned for *Singing the Living Tra-*
>   *dition.*

3   The World Stands Out on Either Side
Edna St. Vincent Millay (1892-1950) was an accomplished poet and dramatist. Born in Rockland, Maine, she was awarded the 1923 Pulitzer Prize for Poetry for "The Ballad of the Harp-Weaver." From the closing section of her poem "Renascence" comes this hymn, which was included in *Hymns for the Celebration of Life*, 1964. *Renascence and Other Poems* was Millay's first book, published in 1917.
>   RICKER. Weldon Frederick Wooden (1953-), one of the compilers of
>   *Singing the Living Tradition*, is a Unitarian Universalist minister
>   serving the First Unitarian Congregational Society, Brooklyn, New
>   York. He has served congregations in Austin, Texas, and Groton
>   and Petersham, Massachusetts. This tune was named in memory
>   of his father-in-law, Roger R. Ricker, Jr.

4   I Brought My Spirit to the Sea
Max Kapp (1904-1979), a Unitarian Universalist minister, served congregations in Massachusetts and New York. From 1942 to 1965 he was professor and dean of the Theological School of Saint Lawrence University. In

1965 he became the director of overseas and interfaith relations for the Unitarian Universalist Association. This text hangs on the wall of the dining room at Camp Ferry Beach in Saco, Maine, where for years it has been sung to the tune, "Drink to Me Only With Thine Eyes."

JACQUI. Alec Wyton (1921-), organist and composer, is a former chair of the Department of Church Music, Manhattan School of Music. This tune was commissioned for *Singing the Living Tradition*.

5　It Is Something to Have Wept

Gilbert Keith Chesterton (1874-1936), controversial British journalist, novelist, and critic, became a Roman Catholic in 1922. This text uses four of the six stanzas, with slight changes, of "The Great Minimum" in *Poems by Gilbert Keith Chesterton*, 1915.

KEITH. Robert L. Sanders (1906-), a Unitarian Universalist, composed this tune for *Hymns for the Celebration of Life*, 1964, of which he was a compiler. While teaching at Chicago Conservatory, the University of Chicago, and Meadville Theological School, Sanders served as organist-director of the First Unitarian Society. In 1937 he cowrote the music preface of *Hymns of the Spirit*. In 1938 he became dean of the School of Music at Indiana University, and from 1947 on he served as professor of music at Brooklyn College.

6　Just as Long as I Have Breath

Alicia S. Carpenter (1930-) is a Unitarian Universalist professional singer and songwriter who lives in Ithaca, New York, and Garden Ridge, Texas.

NICHT SO TRAURIG. Johann Georg Ebeling (1637-1676), music director at the St. Nicholas Church, Berlin, Germany, and professor of music at the Caroline Gymnasium, Stettin, Poland, composed this tune. The harmonization was revised by John Edwin Giles (1949-1996), former director of music at the Unitarian Church of Evanston, Illinois.

7　The Leaf Unfurling

Don Cohen (1946-) is a playwright and computer systems manager who attends the First Parish Church, Lexington, Massachusetts. This text was written in 1980 for the ordination of his wife, the Reverend Helen Lutton Cohen, at the Unitarian Universalist Church in Arlington, Massachusetts. It was originally set to Ralph Vaughan Williams's SINE NOMINE.

ALL LIFE IS ONE. John Corrado (1940-) is a Unitarian Universalist minister who has served congregations in Charleston, West Virginia;

Camp Springs, Maryland; Albany, New York; and currently the Unitarian Church, Grosse Pointe, Michigan.

8 Mother Spirit, Father Spirit

Norbert F. Čapek (1870-1942) was raised as a Baptist in Czechoslovakia. Upon visiting a Unitarian church in Orange, New Jersey, in the 1920s, he found that his beliefs more closely resembled those of the Unitarians. Returning to his native land, he founded the Unitarian Church of Prague, where he served as minister for many years and created the Flower Communion Service. He was killed at Dachau concentration camp in 1942, for speaking out and acting against Nazi persecution. The English version of this text is by Richard Frederick Boeke (1931-), a Unitarian Universalist minister. Boeke was ordained Baptist in 1955 and transferred in 1959. He is minister emeritus of the Sevenoaks Unitarian Church in Kent, England, and also served Unitarian Universalist congregations in Nevada, California, New York, and Florida. His version came from a translation by Paul and Anita Munk.

> MÅTI SVETA. Norbert F. Čapek (1870-1942). This harmonization is by David Dawson (1939-), a lecturer in music education, who attends the Bradford Unitarian Church in Bradford, England. He served as music editor for the British Unitarian hymnbook, *Hymns for Living*, 1985.

9 No Longer Forward nor Behind

John Greenleaf Whittier (1807-1892), poet, Quaker, and abolitionist, was born on a farm near Haverhill, Massachusetts. At least seventy-five selections have been drawn from his poetry for inclusion in hymnbooks. This text is drawn from four stanzas of "My Psalm."

> VAN DIEMAN'S LAND. English folk tune, arranged and edited by Waldemar Hille (1908-1996), a Unitarian Universalist, who attended the First Unitarian Church of Los Angeles, California. He was the editor of the songbook, *How Can We Keep From Singing!*, published by that church in 1976.

10 Immortal Love

John Greenleaf Whittier. *See No. 9.* This hymn consists of stanzas from "Our Master," published in *Tent on the Beach and Other Poems*, 1867. When someone said, "But you, Sir, could never have been a Puritan and a Calvinist," the Quaker poet replied, "Nay, thee is right! The world is much too beautiful, and God much too good. I never was of that mind."

> ST. COLUMBIA is an Irish melody.

11 O God of Stars and Sunlight

John Holmes (1904-1962), a Unitarian, was a poet and from 1934 a professor of English at Tufts University. He wrote many volumes of poetry as well as a book of nonfiction, *Writing Poetry*. This hymn was written for the 1948 meeting of the American Unitarian Association. The text has been slightly revised.

MUNICH is by Felix Mendelssohn (1809-1847).

12 O Life That Maketh All Things New

Samuel Longfellow (1819-1892), the younger brother of the poet Henry Wadsworth Longfellow (*see No. 240*), was an influential hymn writer and editor. Reared in the First Parish Society in Portland, Maine, he became a Unitarian minister, serving churches in Massachusetts, New York, and Pennsylvania. While a student at Harvard Divinity School he edited *A Book of Hymns for Public and Private Devotion*, 1846, with classmate Samuel Johnson. *See No. 111*. That book, which became known as the "Book of Sams," was revised in 1848, and had twelve editions. Other hymnbooks followed, notably *Hymns of the Spirit*, 1864, also edited with Samuel Johnson. The author of some fifty hymns, Longfellow also wrote several biographies. This text, originally titled "The Light that Lighteth Every Man," was first sung at the second Social Festival of the Free Religious Association in 1874. Longfellow and Samuel Johnson devised memorable and expressive synonyms for the word "God": "O Life that maketh all things new," "Light of ages and of nations" (Longfellow); and "Life of ages, richly poured" (Johnson).

> TRURO. This tune appeared in Thomas Williams's *Psalmodia Evangelica*, 1789, as a setting of "Now to the Lord a Noble Song." It is sometimes ascribed, without evidence, to Charles Burney (1726-1814).

13 Songs of Spirit

Marion Franklin Ham (1867-1956) joined the Unitarian church in Chattanooga, Tennessee, where he became a lay leader and was ordained in 1898, without a college education, as its minister. He later served Unitarian churches in Texas and Massachusetts. He published *The Golden Shuttle*, 1896, and several other books of poetry, including *Songs of a Lifetime*, 1953.

> SERVETUS. Thomas Oboe Lee (1945-) is a composer and associate professor of music at Boston College. This tune was commissioned for *Singing the Living Tradition* and is named to commemorate Miguel Servet, often called by his Latin name, Michael Servetus.

His pamphlets decrying the doctrine of the Trinity and his martyr's death at the hands of John Calvin of Geneva inspired many religious radicals during the Reformation.

14   The Sun at High Noon
Sydney Henry Knight (1923-), a British Unitarian minister, served as the Secretary of the British Unitarian Religious Education Department, 1964-1971; a London District Minister, 1976-1986; president of the British General Assembly of Unitarian and Free Christian Churches, 1985-1986; and as the editor of *Songs for Living*, 1972, and *Hymns for Living*, 1985. He is now minister of the St. Saviourgate Unitarian Chapel in York, England. This text was inspired by a nursery school teacher on a nature walk.

MACDOWELL. Thomas Benjamin. *See No. 2.*

15   The Lone, Wild Bird
H. R. MacFayden (1877-1964), the son of a Presbyterian minister, served the Presbyterian Church at Pinetops, North Carolina. This, his only hymn, was written for a hymn-writing contest (at which it was awarded third prize).

PROSPECT. From William Walker's *The Southern Harmony*, 1835. Walker (1809-1875), of Spartanburg, South Carolina, used this tune and others to conduct singing schools in the southeastern states.

16   'Tis a Gift to Be Simple
Joseph Bracket (18th century).

SIMPLE GIFTS. American Shaker tune. "The Shakers" was the nickname of an eighteenth- and nineteenth-century Christian movement led in the US by Mother Ann Lee. The Shakers believed in communal sharing of possessions, pacifism, and equality of the sexes; Shaker worship was spontaneous, with no written prayers, liturgy, or songs.

17   Every Night and Every Morn
William Blake (1757-1827) was a visionary British poet and painter who wrote and illustrated epic poems on religious and mystical themes. His well-known works include *The Marriage of Heaven and Hell* and *Songs of Innocence*. This text is arranged from *Auguries of Innocence*.

THE CALL. Ralph Vaughan Williams's (1872-1958) genius and enthusiasm for folk song brought new life to British hymnody and music. A native of Gloucestershire, Vaughan Williams studied at the Royal College of Music and at Trinity College, Cambridge, where he received a doctorate in music in 1901. Among his teachers were Sir Hubert Parry (*see No. 337*) and Maurice Ravel. His compositions include many choral works and songs, four operas, nine symphonies, and numerous hymns. He was professor of composition at the Royal College of Music, musical editor of *The English Hymnal*, 1906, and co-editor of *The Oxford Book of Carols*, 1928, and *Songs of Praise*, 1925. *Five Mystical Songs from George Herbert*, the composition from which this tune comes, was written in 1911; it was later adapted as a hymn and appeared in *Hymnal for Colleges and Schools*, 1956.

18   What Wondrous Love
This classic US folk hymn from William Walker's *The Southern Harmony*, 1835, is based on a sea chanty about Captain Kidd and displays a Celtic influence. The original words are attributed to the Reverend Alex Means. Several modernizations of the text have been published, including a version in *How Can We Keep From Singing!* This adaptation is by Connie Campbell Hart (1929-), an artist, musician, and member of the First Unitarian Universalist Church of Detroit, Michigan.
    WONDROUS LOVE. Melody from *The Southern Harmony*, 1835, with alternate harmonization by Carlton R. Young (1926-). Young is the editor of the *United Methodist Hymnal*, 1989, and its precursor, *The Methodist Hymnal*, 1966. He is a teacher, composer, conductor, and professor of church music.

19   The Sun That Shines
Dimitri S. Bortniansky (Dmitri Stepanovich Bortnyansky) (1751-1825) wrote the text of verse 1. Director of the Russian imperial court chapel choir, Bortniansky was a successful composer of operas, sacred music, and instrumentals. Verses 2 and 3 are by John Andrew Storey. *See No. 2.*
    BARNFIELD. David Dawson. *See No. 8.*

20   Be Thou My Vision
Ancient Irish. Translated by Mary E. Byrne (1880-1931) and versed by Eleanor H. Hull (1860-1935). This text has been altered.
    SLANE. Traditional Irish melody harmonized by Carlton R. Young. *See No. 18.*

21   For the Beauty of the Earth

Folliott Sandford Pierpoint (1835-1917) was a British classicist and poet. The original text—later altered, as here, by many denominations—included a refrain beginning, "Christ, our God, to thee we raise"; the refrain alluded to one of the earliest secular references to Christians in a letter by Pliny the Younger to the Roman Emperor Trajan, which mentioned Christians gathering before daybreak to repeat in turn "a hymn to Christ as to a god." This nature hymn, originally of eight stanzas, was written for Anglican communion services.

> DIX. Conrad Kocher (1786-1872), director of music in the collegiate church at Stuttgart, Germany, in his *Stimmen aus dem Reiche Gottes*, 1838, published his setting of Zeller's "Treuer Heiland, wir sind hier." This became the tune "Dix," when the third phrase was omitted to accommodate William Chatterton Dix's "As with gladness men of old" in the first musical edition of *Hymns Ancient and Modern*, 1861.

22   Dear Weaver of Our Lives' Design

Nancy Currier Dorian (1936-), a former professor, is a Unitarian Universalist from Brunswick, Maine. This hymn was one of the winners of a competition for hymn texts celebrating feminine imagery of the divine sponsored by the Hymnbook Resources Commission.

> LOBT GOTT, IHR CHRISTEN. Nikolaus Herman (1480-1561), Meistersinger and friend of Martin Luther's, was cantor in Joachimstal, Bohemia. The tune was first found in *Ein Christlicher Abentreien*, Leipzig, Germany, 1554. This version is the closing chorale in Johann Sebastian Bach's (*see No. 200*) Cantata 151, "Süsser Trost, mein Jesus kommt," 1740.

23   Bring Many Names

Brian Wren (1936-), a contemporary hymn writer, was born and educated in England. Ordained a minister in the United Reformed Church, he served local congregations, served on the staff of the British Council of Churches, and worked for Third World First prior to 1983, when he chose to devote himself full-time to hymn writing. He is the author of *Education for Justice*, *What Language Shall I Borrow?*, and several hymn collections, including *Bring Many Names*, *New Beginnings*, and *Piece Together Praise*. His hymns are well represented in Presbyterian, Lutheran, Methodist, and other hymnals and in *Singing the Living Tradition*.

> WESTCHASE. Carlton R. Young. *See No. 18.*

24 Far Rolling Voices

Max Kapp. *See No. 4.*

> OIKOUMENE. I-to Loh (1936-) is a professor of church music and ethnomusicology at Tainen Theological College and at the Asian Institute for Liturgy and Music, Manila, Philippines. He has compiled and edited several music collections, including *A Festival of Asian Christmas Music*, *African Songs of Worship*, *Asian Songs of Worship*, and *Hymns from the Four Winds*. This tune uses three versions of a single tune to exhibit the cultural diversity of Asia, signifying that "in Christ there are indeed East and West."

25 God of the Earth, the Sky, the Sea

Samuel Longfellow. *See No. 12.* This definition of God is reminiscent of that in William Wordsworth's "Tintern Abbey," reprinted as No. 499 of *Singing the Living Tradition*. Longfellow's text was printed anonymously in *Hymns of the Spirit*, 1864. Some revisions have been made.

> DUKE STREET. John Hatton (1710-1793) was a resident of this street in the township of Windle, England. He is not to be confused with another composer, John Liptrott Hatton (1809-1886).

26 Holy, Holy, Holy, Author of Creation

Reginald Heber (1783-1826) was an Anglican cleric, hymn writer, and hymnbook compiler, who became bishop of Calcutta, with all of India as his diocese, in 1823. American Unitarian arrangements of this text, which have omitted Heber's reference to the Trinity, date to at least 1848. The words, "holy, holy, holy," as an address to God appear in Isaiah 6:3, Revelations 4:8, and in the traditional eucharistic prayer of the Christian church from early times.

> NICAEA. John Bacchus Dykes (1823-1876), from Yorkshire, directed the choir of Durham Cathedral and was a founder of the University Musical Society at Cambridge. This tune was composed for *Hymns Ancient and Modern*, 1861. Appropriate to Bishop Heber's original text, the name refers to the Christian ecumenical council at Nicaea in 325 CE, at which the doctrine of the Trinity was formalized.

27 I Am That Great and Fiery Force

Hildegard of Bingen (1098-1179), Abbess of Rupertsberg, was a mystic, poet, composer, and scholar. At an early age she began seeing visions of the relationship between God and humanity in creation, redemption, and the Church; her visions were later authenticated by the archbishop of Mainz and Pope Eugenius III. She founded a convent at Rupertsberg and traveled throughout Gaul and Germany speaking to people of all classes on the prophecies in her visions. Included as a saint in the Roman Martyrology, Hildegard has twice been selected as a candidate for canonization, although the process has never been completed. Twenty-six of her visions are recorded in *Scivias*. She also wrote *Lives of St. Disibod and St. Rupert*, two books of medicine and natural history, and both texts and music for many hymns and canticles.

AVE VERA VIRGINITAS. Josquin Desprez (also des Prés, des Prez) (ca. 1445-1521) was one of the greatest composers of the Renaissance. He is believed to have been born in Condé-sur-l'Escaut, France, but records concerning Desprez's early years are incomplete. As an adult, he served as a singer at Milan Cathedral for thirteen years and at numerous court chapels in France and Italy. His numerous compositions, which contributed to the development of modern harmony, include masses, motets, and secular vocal works. This adaptation is by Anthony Petti (1932-).

28   View the Starry Realm of Heaven

Norbert F. Čapek. *See No. 8.* This hymn was written while he was imprisoned in Dachau. The text was translated by Richard F. Boeke. *See No. 8.*

DACHAU. Bodhana Čapek Haspl, daughter of Norbert F. Čapek and a Unitarian Universalist, wrote this tune. The harmonization is by Betsy Jo Angebranndt (1931-), director of music at the Unitarian Universalist Church of Annapolis, Maryland.

29   Joyful, Joyful, We Adore Thee

Henry Van Dyke (1852-1933) was a US Congregational and Presbyterian minister, professor, and diplomat. He chaired the committees that prepared the North American Presbyterian *Book of Common Worship*, 1905, and its 1932 revision. This hymn was written during a visit to Williams College where Van Dyke said to President James A. Garfield, "Here is a hymn for you. Your mountains were my inspiration. It must be sung to the music of Beethoven's 'Hymn to Joy.'"

HYMN TO JOY. Adapted from the Ninth Symphony of Ludwig van Beethoven (1770-1827), the great German composer whose music bridged the classical and romantic periods. The adaptor, Edward Hodges (1796-1867), was an Englishman who settled in New York in 1839, where he became organist of St. John's Episcopal Chapel and Trinity Church.

30 Over My Head

African American spiritual (ca. 1750-1875). During slavery, African Americans fought a constant battle against psychological as well as physical slavery. Spirituals like this one were sung to rejuvenate the spirit, as well as to remind the oppressors that God would eventually set things right.

> REEB. African American spiritual (ca. 1750-1875), arranged by Horace Clarence Boyer (1935-). The tune is named for James Reeb (1927-1965), a Unitarian Universalist minister who worked for social justice in the Roxbury section of Boston. He was killed following a civil rights march in Selma, Alabama, in 1965.

31 Name Unnamed

Brian Wren. *See No. 23.* Many of the phrases and images in this hymn came from a discussion of images of divinity at the Pacific School of Religion in Berkeley, California.

> SAMUEL. Weldon Frederick Wooden. *See No. 3.* This tune was named in memory of his son, Samuel Daley Wooden.

32 Now Thank We All Our God

Martin Rinkart (1586-1649) was a German pastor, poet, and musician. He served for more than thirty years as priest at Eilenburg. This text consists of the first stanza, the first quatrain of the second stanza, and the second quatrain of the third stanza of Catherine Winkworth's translation of the original, based on Ecclesiastes 50:22-24, which begins, "Nun danket alle Gott." Winkworth (1827-1878), an Anglican, educator, and feminist, was known for her translations of German hymns into English. This text is from her *Lyra Germanica*, Second Series, 1858.

> NUN DANKET ALLE GOTT. Johann Crüger (1598-1662), for forty years cantor at the St. Nicholas Church, Berlin, first published his setting of this tune in *Praxis Pietatis Melica*, 1648. That collection, of which he was an editor, had forty editions by 1724.

33 Sovereign and Transforming Grace

Frederick Henry Hedge (1805-1890), a Unitarian minister and scholar, wrote this hymn for a friend's ordination in 1829, the year he was ordained minister of the First Congregational Parish, West Cambridge (now Arlington), Massachusetts. He later served other Unitarian parishes in Maine, Rhode Island, and Massachusetts. He was a pioneer in introducing current German literature and metaphysics in the United States, and ended his career as professor of German at Harvard.

> MANTON. Jane Manton Marshall (1924-), teacher and composer from

Dallas, Texas, teaches courses in church music at Perkins School of Theology. This tune was commissioned for *Singing the Living Tradition*.

34   Though I May Speak with Bravest Fire
Hal H. Hopson (1933-) is a composer, organist, and choir director in Nashville, Tennessee. This text comes from I Corinthians 13:1-3.
> GIFT OF LOVE. Traditional English melody, adapted by Hal H. Hopson. *See No. 33.*

35   Unto Thy Temple, Lord, We Come
Robert Collyer (1823-1912) was a Yorkshire blacksmith with little formal education who came to America in 1850 as a Methodist preacher. Drawn to Unitarian beliefs through friendship with Dr. W. H. Furness of the First Unitarian Church of Philadelphia, he left the Methodist church and in 1859 was called to the newly organized Unity Unitarian Church in Chicago. He served there for twenty years before going to the Church of the Messiah (now the Community Church), New York, New York. This text was written for the dedication of the new building after the Unity Church building was destroyed in the 1870 Chicago fire. Stanza 3 is omitted here.
> DUKE STREET. John Hatton. *See No. 25.*

36   When In Our Music
Fred Pratt Green (1903-) is a retired British Methodist minister. Inspired by this tune, he wrote this text in 1971.
> ENGELBERG. Charles Villiers Stanford (1852-1924).

37   God Who Fills the Universe
Carl G. Seaburg (1922-), former Directory editor for the Unitarian Universalist Association, is a retired Unitarian Universalist minister. He served congregations in Medford, Massachusetts; North Montpelier and Montpelier, Vermont; and Norway, Maine. He is the editor of *The Communion Book*, 1993; *Celebrating Christmas*, 1983; and *Great Occasions*, 1968. He adapted the text of this widely used Transylvanian Unitarian hymn.
> FRANCIS DÁVID. Transylvanian hymn tune, harmonized by Larry Phillips (1948-), a musician and music director for the First Parish in Waltham, Massachusetts. This tune is named for Francis Dávid (1510-1579), court preacher to John Sigismund (1540-1571), king of Transylvania, the only Unitarian king in history. Dávid's influence on the king's religion was profound, leading the king to issue the first known religious freedom edict in the world. Dávid and his

followers were called "Unitarian," believed to be the first time this term was applied to a religious movement. He was martyred for his beliefs in 1579.

38 Morning Has Broken
Eleanor Farjeon (1881-1965) was a British writer, specializing in works for children, who at the age of seventy was received into the Roman Catholic Church. She wrote this hymn to fit the tune "Bunessan" by request for *Songs of Praise*, 1931.

> BUNESSAN. Gaelic melody from Lachlan Macbean's *Songs and Hymns of the Gael*, 1900, harmonized by David Evans (1872-1948), an academic, church musician, and leader of Welsh national musical life.

39 Bring, O Morn, Thy Music
William Channing Gannett (1840-1923), a Unitarian minister, served congregations in Minnesota and New York, among others, and served briefly as secretary of the Western Unitarian Conference. Written in 1892, this text appeared in *A Chorus of Faith* as an account and résumé of the 1893 World Parliament of Religions in Chicago. The author's title, "Who Wert and Art and Evermore Shalt Be," relates the hymn to Reginald Heber's "Holy, Holy, Holy" (*see No. 26*), for which the tune "Nicaea" was composed.

> NICAEA. John Bacchus Dykes. *See No. 26.*

40 The Morning Hangs a Signal
William Channing Gannett. *See No. 39.* The present text, arranged circa 1930 by Curtis Reese, first appeared in *Love to God and Love to Man*, circa 1885, a collection of liberal texts adapted to popular revival tunes, this one to "The Crowning Day." It was recast by Vincent B. Silliman (*see No. 42*) in 1934 and set to this tune for *The Beacon Song and Service Book*. Additional revisions have been made.

> MEIRIONYDD. William Lloyd (1786-1852), composer, was a Welsh farmer who held singing classes in his home. Called "Berth" in *Caniadau Seion*, a manuscript tune book of 1840, the tune takes this name from Merionethshire, just south of Lloyd's county, Caernarvon. The tune has been slightly revised.

41 You That Have Spent the Silent Night
George Gascoigne (1540-1577) was an English literary pioneer, law student, prodigal, member of Parliament, soldier, satirist, and poet. Here are a stanza and a half from his poem "Gascoigne's Good Morrowe," which in a

later stanza rates our days on earth as "but hell to heavenly joy." The last lines of the text were original to *Hymns for the Celebration of Life*, 1964. The text has been modernized here.

LOBT GOTT, IHR CHRISTEN. Nikolaus Herman. *See No. 22.* Harmony by J. S. Bach (1685-1750), the genius of baroque music. A talented court organist and musician, he composed hundreds of musical works, including nearly 300 cantatas. In his compositions Bach brought counterpoint and fugue to their greatest heights.

42 Morning, So Fair to See

Vincent B. Silliman (1894-1979), a Unitarian Universalist minister, was one of the compilers of *Hymns for the Celebration of Life*, 1964. Born in Hudson, Wisconsin, he served congregations in New York, Maine, and Illinois. He was an editor of *The Beacon Song and Service Book*, 1935; of *We Sing of Life*, 1955, with Irving Lowens; and of *We Speak of Life*, 1955. This text was prepared for *The Beacon Song and Service Book* and is based on a lyric by Bernhardt Severin Ingemann (1789-1862), a Danish Lutheran poet and professor. Here is a version recast in 1991.

SCHÖNESTER HERR JESU. A folk melody from Silesia, a region of central Europe. This tune was used for a preexisting text in A. H. Hoffmann von Fallersleben's *Schlesische Volkslieder*, 1842. Franz Liszt, who used the melody in his oratorio *The Legend of St. Elizabeth*, 1862, fancifully asserted that it was "an old pilgrim song apparently from the Crusades." This tune was harmonized by T. Tertius Noble (1867-1953).

43 The Morning, Noiseless

Anonymous, recast in 1960 and 1990.

NATURE'S ADVENT. William Albright (1944-1998), a Unitarian Universalist, is professor of music composition at the University of Michigan and a performer specializing in recent music for organ. This tune was commissioned by the First Unitarian Universalist Church of Ann Arbor, Michigan, for its 125th anniversary in 1990.

44 We Sing of Golden Mornings

Ralph Waldo Emerson (1803-1882), Unitarian minister and writer, was the founder of the Transcendentalist movement. After graduating from Harvard Divinity School, he became associate minister of the Second Unitarian Church in Boston in 1829. In 1832 he resigned this position because of doubts about the practice of communion. He was an outspoken opponent of slavery and advocate for emancipation. His "Divinity School Address,"

1838, marked the change in American Unitarian thought from Bible and miracle to individual conscience as the final warrant in religion. This hymn text is loosely based on "The World Soul," in Emerson's *Poems*, 1847; a hymn version was published in *Free Religious Hymns*, London, 1925, edited by Walter Walsh as "a hymnal of Universal Religion." Vincent B. Silliman (*see No. 42*) rewrote Walsh's adaptation for *We Sing of Life*, 1955. Here is a version of the hymn recast in 1990.

> COMPLAINER. From William Walker's *The Southern Harmony. See No. 15.*

45   Now While the Day in Trailing Splendor

Frederick Lucian Hosmer (1840-1929) was a Unitarian minister who served congregations in Massachusetts, Illinois, Ohio, Missouri, and California. Beginning in 1875 and continuing for nearly four decades, he and William Channing Gannett (*see No. 39*) worked together, making a contribution to hymnody comparable to that of the "two Sams," Longfellow and Johnson, a generation earlier. It has been said, "Gannett was the better poet, Hosmer the better hymn writer." Written in 1902, this hymn was included in Louisa Loring's *Hymns of the Ages*, 1904.

> LEE. Thomas Oboe Lee. *See No. 13.* This tune was commissioned for *Singing the Living Tradition.*

46   Now the Day Is Over

Sabine Baring-Gould (1834-1924), English minister and author of novels, theological works, and hymns, wrote verse 1. Marye B. Bonney (1910-1992), a Unitarian Universalist and teacher, attended the First Unitarian Church of Louisville, Kentucky.

> WEM IN LEDENSTAGEN. Friedrich Filitz (1804-1860).

47   Now on Land and Sea Descending

Samuel Longfellow. *See No. 12.* This vesper hymn, written in 1859, appears in *Hymns of the Spirit*, 1864.

> VESPER HYMN. Russian melody. This tune was arranged and published in 1818 as a glee for four voices in *A Selection of Popular National Airs* by Sir John A. Stevenson (1761-1833). Stevenson, an Irish musician, called it "Russian Air." It has been ascribed to Dimitri Bortniansky (*see No. 19*), but authoritative support for this assertion is lacking.

48 Again, as Evening's Shadow Falls
Samuel Longfellow. *See No. 12.* This hymn was originally published in *Vespers*, 1859, a collection for use in services that Longfellow instituted in Brooklyn, New York.

ROCKBRIDGE. Amzi Chapin (1768-), cabinetmaker and singing master, was born into a prominent musical family in North Carolina. Many a tune is attributed to "Chapin," although it is unclear which member of the family composed it.

49 Stillness Reigns
Guttormur J. Guttormsson, an Icelandic Unitarian, was a farmer and a poet. He lived in the Manitoba Interlake district of Canada.

QUEM PASTORES. German tune (ca. 1400), harmonized by Ralph Vaughan Williams. *See No. 17.*

50 When Darkness Nears
Philip A. Porter (1953-) is an artist, writer, and performer who codirects an improvisational dance group in the San Francisco Bay area. Active in the United Church of Christ, he has performed at many Unitarian Universalist gatherings.

DOVER KNIGHT. David Hurd (1950-) is professor of church music and organist at the General Theological Seminary of the Episcopal Church, New York. He served as assistant organist of the Trinity Parish in Lower Manhattan; professor in the graduate studies programs of the University of North Carolina, Chapel Hill, and Duke University, and as organist and music director at the Chapel of the Intercession. His liturgical compositions and arrangements are found in several recent hymnals.

51 Lady of the Seasons' Laughter
Kendyl L. R. Gibbons (1955-) is a Unitarian Universalist minister serving the DuPage Unitarian Church in Naperville, Illinois. This text won a competition for hymn texts celebrating feminine imagery of the divine sponsored by the Hymnbook Resources Commission.

JULION. David Hurd. *See No. 50.*

52 In Sweet Fields of Autumn
Elizabeth Syle Madison (b. 1883) lived in Salinas, California. This text was first published in *Hymns for the Celebration of Life,* 1964.

CRADLE SONG. William James Kirkpatrick (1838-1921) was an Irish-born carpenter, music director of Grace Methodist Episcopal Church in Philadelphia, and publisher of popular gospel song collections. This tune, a setting of "Away in a Manger," was published in *Around the World with Christmas*, 1895, and harmonized by Ralph Vaughan Williams in 1931. *See No. 17.*

53   I Walk the Unfrequented Road
Frederick Lucian Hosmer. *See No. 45.* This poem's date of composition is unknown, but its first publication in a hymnbook is believed to be in Stanton Coit's *Social Worship II*, London, 1913.

> CONSOLATION. John Wyeth (1770-1858) was a Unitarian from Cambridge, Massachusetts. This tune is from his *Repository of Sacred Music, II*, 1813, which was prepared for Methodists and Baptists to the west and south.

54   Now Light Is Less
Theodore Huebner Roethke (1908-1963), once dubbed the greatest American reader, was an award-winning poet and educator. Born in Saginaw, Michigan, he taught for thirteen years at the University of Washington in Seattle. In 1954 he won the Pulitzer Prize for *The Waking: Poems 1933-1953*. Many of his poems have been set to music, including "The Serpent" and several poems from *I Am! Says the Lamb*, 1961. This text is from "The Slow Season."

> SURSUM CORDA. Alfred Morton Smith (1879-1971) was an Episcopal priest and military chaplain. This tune appeared in *The Hymnal*, 1940, as the setting for "Lift up your hearts! We lift them, Lord, to thee," written by Henry Montagu Butler.

55   Dark of Winter
Shelley Jackson Denham (1950-) is a Unitarian Universalist and the director of extension and worship at The Mountain, a Unitarian Universalist camp and conference center in Highlands, North Carolina. This text was written to celebrate positive imagery of night and darkness.

> WINTER MEDITATION. Shelley Jackson Denham (1950-).

56   Bells in the High Tower
Howard Box (1926-) is a retired Unitarian Universalist minister who served congregations in Pennsylvania, New York, Ontario, and Oak Ridge, Tennessee, where he is minister emeritus. He was formerly a leader at the Brooklyn Society for Ethical Culture. This text was written for the Unitarian Church of Ottawa's Christmas Sunday, 1958, to accompany this tune.

> KRISZTUS URUNKNAK. Traditional Hungarian carol.

57   All Beautiful the March of Days
Frances Whitmarsh Wile (1878-1939), a Unitarian, wrote this hymn circa 1907 in consultation with the Reverend William Channing Gannett (*see No. 39*) in Rochester, New York. It was included in *Unity Hymns and Chorals*, 1911.

> FOREST GREEN. English melody harmonized in 1906 by Ralph Vaughan Williams. *See No. 17.*

58   Ring Out, Wild Bells
Alfred, Lord Tennyson (1809-1892) was Britain's poet laureate from 1850 until his death and the major figure of poetry's Victorian age. This text includes five of the eight stanzas of Section 106 of "In Memoriam." In the last line, "light" is substituted for "Christ."

> GONFALON ROYAL. Percy Carter Buck (1871-1947), an English music writer, music editor, teacher, and organist, was knighted in 1937 for his service to the English music world. During his long career he served as organist of Wells and Bristol Cathedrals; director of music at the Harrow School; and professor of music at Trinity College, Dublin, and the University of London. His books include *The Oxford History of Music*, *The Oxford Song Book*, and *The Oxford Nursery Song Book*.

59   Almond Trees, Renewed in Bloom
Fred Kaan (1929-) is a Dutch-born minister and hymn writer. He has served as general secretary of the International Congregational Council in Geneva and as executive secretary of the World Alliance of Reformed Churches. He edited the four-language *Reformed Press Service*, chaired the Council for World Mission, and published five collections of hymns, including *Break Not the Circle*, 1975, and *The Hymn Texts of Fred Kaan*, 1985.

> CON X'OM LANG. Nguyen-Duc Quang.

60   In Time of Silver Rain
Langston Hughes (1902-1967) was a leading African American poet and writer from the 1920s until his death. Educated at Lincoln and Columbia universities, he was the first Black American to earn a living solely from writing and public lectures. His oeuvre includes poems, translations, newspaper columns, short stories, and several works for the stage. This text is an excerpt from "In Time of Silver Rain," which appears in *Selected Poems of Langston Hughes*.

> LANGSTON. George Theophilus Walker (1922-), a composer and pia-

nist, lives in Montclair, New Jersey. This tune was commissioned for *Singing the Living Tradition*.

61   Lo, the Earth Awakes Again

Samuel Longfellow. *See No. 12*. Here is Longfellow's text as revised by the editors of *Hymns for the Celebration of Life*, 1964, chiefly a rearrangement of lines from stanzas 3 and 4 into a new stanza.

EASTER HYMN. This tune, with its alleluias, is the result of "a desire for a little freer air than the grand movement of the Psalm tunes," according to the anonymous editor of *Lyra Davidica*, 1708, for the text, "Jesus Christ is risen today, Halle-halle-lujah." This form of the tune is from John Arnold's *Compleat Psalmodist*, second edition, 1749. The ascription to Dr. John Worgan is false, because he was not born until 1724.

62   When the Daffodils Arrive

Carl G. Seaburg. *See No. 37*. This text was commissioned for *Singing the Living Tradition*.

HASIDIM. Hasidic tune. Hasidism is an orthodox Jewish movement, founded in eastern Europe in the eighteenth century, that encourages joyous religious expression through song and dance.

63   Spring Has Now Unwrapped the Flowers

Piae Cantiones (1582). This is a translation for *The Oxford Book of Carols*, 1928, of "Tempus adest floridum." "Unfortunately," writes Percy Dearmer in *Songs of Praise Discussed*, "when that unique Swedish book [*Piae Cantiones*] was brought to England and given to Dr. Neale, the latter wrote for it the words of 'Good King Wenceslas,' a poor ballad, difficult to understand, and unworthy of the writer of so many good carols. Habits are difficult to break, but we may hope that gradually the tune will become less associated with Christmas (for which there are so many glorious carols without it), and increasingly sung to its proper spring theme."

BLACKBURN. Thomas Benjamin. *See No. 2*.

64   Oh, Give Us Pleasure in the Flowers Today

Robert Frost (1875-1963) was a New England poet of simple, colloquial verse. He was awarded the Pulitzer Prize for *New Hampshire* in 1924, for *Collected Poems* in 1931, and for *A Further Range* in 1937. He served as professor of poetry at Amherst College for many years, and also taught at Harvard. This text comes from Frost's first collection of poems, *A Boy's Will*, 1913.

COOLINGE. Cyril Vincent Taylor (1907-1991), Anglican theologian and musician, was one of the compilers of the *Hymn Book*, 1951. He was warden of the Royal School of Church Music and author of *The Way to Heaven's Door*, 1955, and *A Chronicle of Carols*, 1957. He also edited *The Botsford Book of Christmas Carols*, 1957.

65 The Sweet June Days

Samuel Longfellow. *See No. 12.* In *Hymns and Verses by Samuel Longfellow*, 1893, this poem is called "Summer Rural Gathering" and dated 1859, with each stanza beginning, "The sweet June days are come again." *Hymns of the Spirit*, 1864, includes stanzas 2 and 3, beginning with, "The summer days are come again" and the concluding quatrain rewritten. Here we have the original opening line, but the final quatrain is revised.

FOREST GREEN. English melody, arranged by Ralph Vaughan Williams. *See No. 17.*

66 When the Summer Sun Is Shining

Sydney Henry Knight. *See No. 14.* This text first appeared in *Songs for Living*, 1972.

HOLY MANNA. From William Walker's *The Southern Harmony*, 1855. *See No. 15.* The accompaniment is by Margaret W. Mealy (1922-).

67 We Sing Now Together

Edwin T. Buehrer (1894-1969), born in Phillipsburg, Texas, was ordained into the Methodist ministry in 1921. In 1941, on Pearl Harbor Day, he changed affiliation and became minister of Third Unitarian Church of Chicago. He served several different denominational churches in Texas, New Jersey, and Maine. He was editor of the *Journal of Liberal Religion* from 1944 to 1947, and president of the Western Unitarian Conference from 1953 to 1959. Here the text has been slightly revised.

KREMSER. Dutch folk tune first published in Adrian Valerius's *Nederlandtsch Gedenckclanck*, 1626, with the text, "Wilt heden nu treden," celebrating the sixteenth-century liberation from Spain. Edward Kremser (1838-1914), director of the Vienna *Männergesangverein*, arranged this tune for men's chorus and orchestra. The 1895 US edition of his *Sechs altniederländische Volkslieder* introduced it to the United States.

68   Come, Ye Thankful People

Henry Alford (1810-1871), an Anglican cleric, became dean of Canterbury in 1857. His magnum opus was *A Greek Testament*, a standard critical commentary of his time. He also published sermons, poems, and hymns, of which only this one is still widely used. This text has been revised.

ST. GEORGE'S WINDSOR. Sir George Job Elvey (1816-1893) was a choirboy at Canterbury Cathedral, and a pupil of Dr. William Crotch (*see No. 113*) at the Royal Academy of Music. From 1835 to 1882 he served as organist and master of the boys at St. George's Chapel, Windsor. This tune was first published in *A Selection of Psalm and Hymn Tunes*, 1858. Since the first musical edition of *Hymns Ancient and Modern*, 1861, it has been associated with "Come, ye thankful people, come."

69   Give Thanks

Anonymous. The original, dating from 1904 or earlier, begins, "For the hay and the corn and the wheat that is reaped." It has been appearing for more than eighty years with no indication of origin. Recast in 1955 and 1989, it was first published in *We Sing of Life*, 1955.

FOUNDATION. From William Caldwell's *Union Harmony*, 1837, and White and King's *Sacred Harp*, 1844. The former calls it "Protection," the latter, "Bellevue," and attributes it to "Z. Chambless" (Chambers?). Some later editors erroneously ascribed it to the poet Anne Steele.

70   Heap High the Farmer's Wintry Hoard

John Greenleaf Whittier. *See No. 9.* This text is an excerpt from "The Huskers."

LAND OF REST. US folk melody arranged by Annabel Morris Buchanan (1888-1983), teacher, composer, and folklorist. Buchanan was the author of *Folk Hymns of America*, 1938, and editor of *White Top Folk Song Series* and *Early American Psalmody*. This tune was harmonized by Charles H. Webb (1933-), an American pianist, conductor, and educator who became dean of the Indiana University School of Music. He and Wallace Hornbook toured the United States in duorecitals. In 1967, Webb was appointed conductor of the Indianapolis Symphony Choir.

71   In the Spring with Plow and Harrow

John Andrew Storey. *See No. 2.*

HEATON. David Dawson. *See No. 8.*

72　Has Summer Come Now, Dawning
Jeanne C. Maki (1943-), a communications and publications consultant who attends the First Universalist Church of Minneapolis, translated this text into English from Finnish.

> CHRISTMAS DAWN. German folk song (1823).

73　Chant for the Seasons
Mark L. Belletini (1949-), chair of the *Singing the Living Tradition* hymnbook commission, is a Unitarian Universalist minister, artist, and author who serves the Starr King Unitarian Church in Hayward, California. He wrote this text for the Hayward congregation because few songs or hymns celebrate the milder seasons.

> PRAHA. Czech folk song, arranged by Grace Lewis-McLaren (1939-), a composer, organist, writer, and editor. She serves as administrative assistant at the First Unitarian Universalist Church of San Diego, California.

74　On the Dusty Earth Drum
Joseph S. Cotter Jr. (1895-1919) was born in Louisville, Kentucky. He attended Fisk University, but left in his second year when he developed tuberculosis. Most of his poetry was written during the six years of his illness, beginning in 1913. His poetry has earned him a high place in the ranks of post-World War I African American poets. He published one volume of poetry, *The Band of Gideon*, 1918, which included this poem.

> WEM IN LEDENSTAGEN. Friedrich Filitz. *See No. 46.*

75　The Harp at Nature's Advent
John Greenleaf Whittier. *See No. 9.* This text is from "The Worship of Nature" and has been slightly altered.

> WALDEN. Jane Manton Marshall. *See No. 33.*

76　For Flowers That Bloom about Our Feet
Anonymous (1904 or earlier). In circulation for more than eighty years, this text is often attributed erroneously to Ralph Waldo Emerson. The original text is altered here.

> WAS GOTT THUT. Severus Gastorius (ca. 1675), cantor at Jena, Germany, wrote this tune to accompany a text written for him by S. Rodigast beginning "Was Gott thut," when Gastorius was sick. This tune was edited by A. Waggoner.

77　Seek Not Afar for Beauty

Minot Judson Savage (1841-1918) was born to orthodox Maine Congrega-
tionalists. After graduating from Bangor Theological Seminary, he served
Congregational churches in California, Massachusetts, and Missouri. In
1872, having read Charles Darwin and Herbert Spencer, he became Unitarian, and subsequently held long pastorates at Boston's Unity Church and
New York's Church of the Messiah (The Community Church). An early
advocate of a religious interpretation of the doctrine of evolution, he wrote
many books. In 1883 he published *Sacred Songs for Public Worship*, containing forty-two of his hymns, only a few of which survive in modern
hymnbooks. Stanzas 2 and 3 have been revised.

> COOLINGE. Cyril Vincent Taylor. *See No. 64.*

78　Color and Fragrance

Norbert F. Čapek. *See No. 8.* The English version of this text, which is
drawn from a translation by Paul and Anita Munk (*see No. 8*), is by Grace
Ulp (1926-), who attends the First Unitarian Church of Berkeley, California.

> O BARVY VUNE. Norbert F. Čapek. *See No. 8.*

79　No Number Tallies Nature Up

Ralph Waldo Emerson. *See No. 44.* This text is adapted from Emerson's
"Song of Nature."

> RESIGNATION. From John W. Steffey's *The Valley Harmonist,* 1836.
> This harmony is by Dale Grotenhuis (1931-).

80　Wild Waves of Storm

Sydney Henry Knight. *See No. 14.* This text was written to accompany the
tune COME LABOR ON for *Hymns for Living,* 1985.

> WILD WAVES. Libby Larsen (1950-) is a composer who lives in Minne-
> apolis, Minnesota. This tune was commissioned for *Singing the
> Living Tradition.*

81　The Wordless Mountains Bravely Still

Philip A. Porter. *See No. 50.*

> BROMLEY. Franz Joseph Haydn (1732-1809), born in Rohrau, Austria,
> began as a choirboy at St. Stephen's, Vienna. For many years he
> served the Esterhazy family as composer and director of music.
> The most famous composer of his day, he wrote more than one
> hundred symphonies and a whole literature of chamber music. He
> composed this grand melody, "Gott erhalte Franz den Kaiser," in

1797 to give his nation an equivalent of "God Save the King." Later he set it with variations as the slow movement of his "Emperor" quartet.

82   This Land of Bursting Sunrise

John Haynes Holmes (1879-1964), a Unitarian Universalist, was minister of the Community Church, New York, New York, for more than fifty years. Author of twenty-one books and many hymns, he is best known for his fiery sermons on social justice and for his work in founding the National Association for the Advancement of Colored People, the American Civil Liberties Union, and the Unitarian Universalist Fellowship for Social Justice. He received the American Unitarian Association's Award for Distinguished Service in 1954. This text was adapted by David Johnson (1943-), a Unitarian Universalist minister who has served congregations in Pittsburgh, Pennsylvania; Tucson, Arizona; and, currently, Brookline, Massachusetts.

ANDUJAR. David Hurd. *See No. 50.*

83   Winds Be Still

Richard S. Kimball (1934-), writer, editor, photographer, and teacher, attends the Allen Avenue Unitarian Universalist Church in Portland, Maine.

LEAD ME LORD. Samuel Sebastian Wesley (1810-1876) was the grandson of Charles Wesley (*see No. 268*) and one of England's greatest church musicians. This tune was written as part of a longer anthem.

84   How Far Can Reach a Smile?

Marjorie Jillson (1931-).

ZIMMERMANN. Heinz Werner Zimmermann, composer (1930-).

85   Although This Life Is But a Wraith

Louis Untermeyer. *See No. 1.* This prayer was included in Untermeyer's *Challenge*, 1914.

DUNEDIN. Vernon Griffiths (b. 1894) was a composer, author, and educator. Born in Chester, England, Griffiths taught music in many institutions in England and New Zealand. He wrote several books on music education, including *An Experiment in School Music Making*; *Music in New Zealand, 1931-37*; and *Music in Education*.

86 Blessed Spirit of My Life

Shelley Jackson Denham. *See No. 55.* This text was written as a prayer.

PRAYER. Shelley Jackson Denham. *See No. 55.*

87 Nearer, My God, to Thee

Sarah Flower Adams (1805-1848), a British Unitarian, wrote this beloved text, based on Genesis 28:10-22, for the Reverend W. H. Fox's *Hymns and Anthems*, 1841. This hymn is sung in translations throughout Christendom.

BETHANY. Lowell Mason (1792-1872), a native of Medfield, Massachusetts, was the leading US church musician of his generation. With the support of Boston's mayor, Samuel Eliot, he founded the Boston Academy of Music in 1832 and introduced music to the public schools in 1838. This tune, composed in 1856, was published in the *Andover Sabbath Hymn and Tune Book*, 1859. Mason said that one night the melody came to him "through the stillness in the house."

88 Calm Soul of All Things

Matthew Arnold (1822-1888) was a British poet and critic who exerted a wide influence on religion and morals by the nobility, grace, and power of his verse. He was professor of poetry at Oxford from 1857 to 1867. This text is from "Lines Written in Kensington Garden."

TALLIS' CANON. Thomas Tallis (ca. 1505-1585), one of the first to compose church music for English as well as Latin texts, was a gentleman of the Chapel Royal throughout the reigns of Henry VIII, Edward VI, Mary, and Elizabeth I. He was organist with William Byrd, with whom he held a monopoly for printing music and ruled music paper in England. This tune has a long history, from its appearance in Archbishop Matthew Parker's *Psalter*, ca. 1561, to its use for congregational participation in Benjamin Britten's miracle play, *Noye's Fludde*, 1957. Note the strict canon between the soprano and tenor parts.

89 Come, My Way, My Truth, My Life

George Herbert (1593-1633), English poet and courtier under James I, took holy orders and in 1630 became rector of Bemerton in Wiltshire, England, where he died. His book of religious verse, *The Temple*, contained this text.

THE CALL. Ralph Vaughan Williams. *See No. 17.*

90   From All the Fret and Fever of the Day

Monroe Beardsley (b. 1915), a Unitarian, was a professor of philosophy at Swarthmore College. He wrote many books on aesthetics, philosophy, and literature. He wrote these stanzas for the Unitarian Church of Delaware County, Springfield, Pennsylvania, for a service designed to show the meaning of silence.

> COOLINGE. Cyril Vincent Taylor. *See No. 64.*

91   Mother of All

Alexander Pope (1688-1744), an English poet and satirist, was the outstanding literary figure of his time. A Roman Catholic, he wrote "Essay on Man," alleged to be an apology for freethinkers. "The Universal Prayer," written as a conclusion to the essay to vindicate his orthodoxy, was in the spirit of the contemporary Deism, which helped shape both American liberties and Unitarian Universalism. Based upon the Lord's Prayer, the piece equates the Christian God with love, honors devout pagans along with Christians, and expresses "natural," rather than revealed, religion. This text uses Pope's verse 1 recast by Michael G. Young, and verses 2, 3, and 4 written by Young (1939-), a Unitarian Universalist minister who has served congregations in California, Florida, and Hawaii.

> ST. COLUMBA. Irish melody also used in No. 10.

92   Mysterious Presence, Source of All

Seth Curtis Beach (1837-1932), a Unitarian minister, served congregations in Maine and Massachusetts. He wrote this hymn for Visitation Day at Harvard Divinity School in 1866, his graduation year.

> WAREHAM. William Knapp (1698-1768) composed this tune, which appeared in his *Sett of New Psalms and Anthems in Four Parts,* 1738. "A country psalm-singer," possibly of German heritage, he was born in Wareham, Dorsetshire, England, and served thirty-nine years as parish clerk of St. James's Church in Poole. There, a local rhymster placed "Will Knapp" as the ultimate terror from which he prayed to be delivered.

93   To Mercy, Pity, Peace, and Love

William Blake. *See No. 17.* This text is excerpted from "The Divine Image" in *Songs of Innocence,* 1789. It first appeared in a hymnbook in *The English Hymnal,* 1906; here the final stanza of the adaptation is omitted.

> LOBT GOTT, IHR CHRISTEN. Nikolaus Herman. *See No. 22.* Harmony by J. S. Bach. *See No. 41.*

94   What Is This Life
William Henry Davies (1871-1940) was a Welsh-born English poet of simple
lyrics on nature, traditional in form. A hobo and peddler by choice as a
young man, he shipped on cattle boats many times to America. After los-
ing a foot under a Canadian freight train in 1901, he became a poet. His
Collected Poems appeared in 1916, 1923, and 1929; his *Autobiography of a
Super-Tramp*, 1907, was called "splendid, rough, simple, direct prose."
> DEVOTION. Closely resembling some British ballad tunes and Gaelic
> melodies, this tune appeared in Allen D. Carden's *Missouri Har-
> mony*, 1820. It was later ascribed to Americk Hall (1785-1827), a
> Massachusetts farmer who manufactured straw bonnets, kept a
> hotel, and taught at a singing school.

95   There Is More Love Somewhere
African American hymn.
> BIKO. African American tune. This tune is named for Steven Bantu
> Biko (1946-1977), a Black South African activist and founder of the
> South African Students' Organization. Threatened by the spread of
> Black consciousness, the government arrested Biko under the Ter-
> rorism Act; he was beaten to death during twenty-two hours of
> interrogation.

96   I Cannot Think of Them as Dead
Frederick Lucian Hosmer. *See No. 45*. This poem, written in 1882, appeared
in *The Thought of God*, 1885, as "My Dead."
> DISTANT BELOVED. W. Frederick Wooden. *See No. 3*. This tune was
> named for one of Beethoven's song cycles, "An Die Ferne Geliebte."

97   Sometimes I Feel Like a Motherless Child
African American spiritual (ca. 1750-1875). It was common practice during slavery for children to be sold away from their parents. This spiritual
was sung as an expression of the anguish and loss many Africans felt as
their families and lives were torn apart and sold off, as well as in sympathy
for the families of the oppressors, many of whom were controlled and destroyed by the practices of slavery.
> WHEATLEY. African American spiritual (ca. 1750-1875). This tune is
> named for Phillis Wheatley (ca. 1753-1784), a Boston African Ameri-
> can poet; her book, *Poems on Various Subjects, Religious and Moral*,
> was published in 1773.

98   Loveliest of Trees
A. E. (Alfred Edward) Housman (1859-1936) was an English poet whose works were often used as lyrics. Born in Fockbury, Worcestershire, he became a professor of Latin at University College in London and Cambridge University. Evoking the transience of beauty and death, Housman's collections *A Shropshire Lad*, 1896, and *Last Poems*, 1922, were favorites among musicians during the English musical revival.
> ORIENTIS PARTIBUS. Medieval French melody harmonized by Carlton R. Young. *See No. 18.*

99   Nobody Knows the Trouble I've Seen
African American spiritual (ca. 1750-1875), believed to have originated after Emancipation and during Reconstruction when freed slaves were uncertain about their status. According to Miles Mark Fisher, author of *Negro Slave Songs in the United States*, 1953, the singer was trying to keep spirits high. Arthur C. Jones, author of *Wade in the Water: The Wisdom of the Spirituals*, 1991, explains that this song was written to provide spiritual hope and the knowledge that God knew what the former slaves had endured and would set things right in the end.
> DUBOIS. African American spiritual (ca. 1750-1875). This tune is named for W. E. B. Du Bois. *See No. 494.*

100   I've Got Peace Like a River
Marvin V. Frey (1918-1992) wrote verses 1, 2, and 3 of this text. Frey, a minister, composed more than 2,000 gospel choruses and hymns. In his youth he served as pianist to many of the most famous evangelists of the late 1930s, including Aimee Semple McPherson, Charles Price, and Emma Cotton. He claimed to have been the original composer of many of the most widely sung gospel choruses in North America today including "Do Lord" and "Kum Ba Yah," although these claims were highly controversial. Verses 4, 5, and 6 are by an anonymous author.
> WHITNEY. Marvin V. Frey (1918-1992).

101   Abide with Me
Henry Francis Lyte (1793-1847), born in Scotland and educated in Ireland, was an Anglican curate for twenty-four years at Lower Brixham, Devonshire, England. Author of several volumes of poetry, he is chiefly remembered for this hymn of approaching death. Long supposed to have been written near the end of his life, it is now believed to have been written around 1820, after a visit to a dying friend, William A. Le Huntte, who repeated the phrase, "Abide with me."

EVENTIDE. William Henry Monk (1823-1889), a London organist and professor of vocal music, was musical coadjutor for the first two editions of *Hymns Ancient and Modern* and musical editor of the enlarged edition of 1875. This setting of the tune was composed for *Hymns Ancient and Modern*, 1861.

102   We the Heirs of Many Ages
John Andrew Storey. *See No. 2.*

BENG-LI. I-to Loh. *See No. 24.* This tune was originally written for the Last Supper scene in a passion play.

103   For All the Saints
William Walsham How (1823-1897), Anglican cleric and bishop of Wakefield, England, edited three hymnals and wrote numerous hymns. This hymn, his most famous, was published with eleven stanzas in Earl Nelson's *Hymns for Saints' Days*, 1864, as "For all thy saints."

SINE NOMINE. Ralph Vaughan Williams (*see No. 17*) composed this tune for *The English Hymnal*, 1906, to replace Sir Joseph Barnby's "St. Philip." The latter was so well entrenched that it is said that a bishop exclaimed on hearing SINE NOMINE, "Good gracious, they will change the tune of 'God Save the King' next!"

104   When Israel Was in Egypt Land
African American spiritual (ca. 1750-1875).

TUBMAN. African American spiritual (ca. 1750-1875). This tune is named for Harriet Tubman (ca. 1821-1913), fugitive slave, abolitionist, army nurse, and Union spy. After her own escape to the north with her two brothers in 1849, she made many journeys back into the South to help other slaves escape to freedom.

105   From Age to Age
Frederick Lucian Hosmer. *See No. 45.* This text was written for the annual festival of the Free Religious Association, June 2, 1899, in Boston. It was published that year in *Souvenir Festival Hymns*.

BENNINGTON. Thomas Benjamin. *See No. 2.*

106   Who Would True Valor See
John Bunyan (1628-1688) was a British pastor, writer, and Nonconformist who spent twelve years in jail for "the crime of preaching." He wrote prolifically, but is best remembered for *Pilgrim's Progress*, 1678. This text appears in the chapter, "Mr. Valiant for Truth," in the 1684 edition. Here

the last stanza substitutes "No word of foe or friend" for "Hobgoblin nor foul fiend." Thus modified, the text was first used as a hymn in *The Beacon Song and Service Book*, 1935.

MONKS GATE. English melody. This tune was collected from a folksinger at Monks Gate near Horsham, Sussex, by Ralph Vaughan Williams (*see No. 17*), who arranged it for *The English Hymnal*, 1906.

107   Now Sing We of the Brave of Old

Albert M. P. Dawson (1880-1963).

VICTORY. Giovanni Pierluigi da Palestrina (ca. 1525-1594) was the most distinguished composer of the Renaissance. Born in Palestrina, Italy, he served as choirmaster, organist, and music master at numerous cathedrals and, briefly, as a member of the papal choir at the Sistine Chapel. He composed more than one hundred masses and many other pieces of sacred choral music. This tune was adapted by William Henry Monk. *See No. 101.*

108   My Life Flows On in Endless Song

Gospel hymn and third verse by Doris Plenn, who wrote this during the McCarthy era, when those who refused to sign loyalty oaths often lost their jobs.

SINGING. Robert Lowry (1826-1899).

109   As We Come Marching, Marching

James Oppenheim (1882-1932), US poet and writer, was born in St. Paul, Minnesota. While working as a teacher and school superintendent, Oppenheim wrote short stories and novels that illuminated the social life of the populace and expressed themes of social justice, transcendental idealism, and poverty. His many works include *The Nine-Tenths*, 1911, and *Pay Envelopes: Tales of the Mill, the Mine and the City Street*, 1911. This text was inspired by a banner during the massive 1912 walkout of textile workers in Lawrence, Massachusetts.

BREAD AND ROSES. Caroline Kohlsaat. Harmonized by Betty A. Wylder (1923-1994), a composer, arranger, and writer who attended the Long Beach, California, Unitarian Universalist Church.

110   Come, Children of Tomorrow

Zona Gale (1874-1938), US writer, spent most of her life in Portage, Wisconsin. She was awarded the Pulitzer Prize for Drama in 1921 for *Miss Lulu Bett*.

VOM HIMMEL HOCH. Martin Luther (*see No. 200*) contributed two prefaces to Valentin Schumann's *Geistliche Lieder*, 1539, which introduced this setting of Luther's text. It has been suggested, without proof, that Luther also wrote the tune. This tune was harmonized by Hans Leo Hassler (1564-1612), a native of Nuremberg, Germany. He studied with Andrea Gabrieli in Venice, and was organist to Octavian Fugger in Augsburg and Prince Christian II in Dresden.

111   Life of Ages

Samuel Johnson (1822-1882), a US minister, Unitarian in belief and closely associated with Unitarian churches, preferred not to be identified with any denomination. From 1853 to 1870 he served the Independent Church of Lynn, Massachusetts, which he organized. With Samuel Longfellow (*see No. 12*) he compiled the influential *A Book of Hymns for Public and Private Devotion*, 1846, revised 1848. This text was one of seven of his in *Hymns of the Spirit*, 1864, which he edited with Longfellow.

VIENNA. Justin Heinrich Knecht (1752-1817), music director at Biberach, Württemberg, Germany, and director of opera and court concerts at Stuttgart, composed this tune. It was first published in *Vollständige Sammlung...für das neue wirtembergische Landgesangbuch*, Stuttgart, 1799, with the text, "Ohne Rast und unverweilt."

112   Do You Hear?

Emily L. Thorn (1915-) is a religious educator who attends the First Unitarian Society of Wilmington, Delaware. She wrote this text to accompany the tune FOUNDATION for year-round, not just Thanksgiving, use.

FOUNDATION. *See No. 69.* This harmony is by Eugene Wilson Hancock (1929-), director of music, West End Presbyterian Church, New York, New York. He is the author and performer of *Organ Music of Black Composers*.

113   Where Is Our Holy Church?

Edwin Henry Wilson (1898-1993), a Unitarian minister, served congregations in Illinois, New York, Utah, Florida, and Ohio. He was one of the principal founders of American religious humanism, serving as the first editor, in 1928, of *The New Humanist* magazine and the first editor, in 1941, of *The Humanist*. In 1941, with philosopher John Dewey and others, he founded the American Humanist Association, of which he was executive director from 1949 to 1970. In 1978 he received the Unitarian Universalist Association's Award for Distinguished Service. He wrote this hymn in the year of his ordination, 1928, and it was first published in *The New Humanist*.

> ST. MICHAEL. Abridged from the 1551 Genevan setting of Psalm 101, this tune was used in English and Scottish psalmody as "Old 134th." This version, adapted by William Crotch (1775-1847), appeared in his *Psalm Tunes*, 1836. Crotch was the first principal of the Royal Academy of Music, London, and a composer of many works for organ and piano.

114   Forward through the Ages

Frederick Lucian Hosmer. *See No. 45.*

> ST. GERTRUDE. Sir Arthur Seymour Sullivan (1842-1900) composed this tune, published in the *Hymnary*, 1872, for "Onward, Christian Soldiers," Sabine Baring-Gould's (*see No. 46*) text for a children's festival. Sullivan is best known for the popular operettas he composed with librettist Sir William Gilbert. The first to hold the Mendelssohn Scholarship at the Royal Academy of Music, Sullivan eventually became professor of music there. In addition to works for the stage, he composed cantatas, ballads, hymn tunes, and an opera.

115   God of Grace and God of Glory

Harry Emerson Fosdick (1878-1969) was a Baptist minister and author of many books. Originally a Presbyterian, after a heresy trial he became minister of what is now the Riverside Church in New York City and was radio minister to Protestants throughout the country. This text was written in 1930 for the dedication of the Riverside Church.

> CWM RHONDDA. John Hughes (1873-1932). This tune stands for many as the archetypal Welsh hymn tune. Hughes, a railroad clerk by profession, was active as a deacon and a leader of singing with the Baptists throughout his life. He composed many other popular hymn tunes.

116   I'm On My Way

African American folk hymn. Many of the African American spirituals sung today were "map songs" that gave coded directions to safety zones or the underground railroad for runaway slaves. Many spirituals and folk songs created during slavery passed along messages of secret meetings, family ties, warning, and escape. This song is believed to be an announcement of an escape attempt and an invitation to join. The success of such songs was based primarily on the secret messages concealed in lines of religious piety.

ETHELRED. Traditional African American folk hymn (ca. 1750-1875). The Hymnbook Resources Commission named this tune in honor of Egbert Ethelred Brown (1875-1956), the first African American to be ordained a Unitarian minister in 1912. This arrangement is by Mary Allen Walden (1946-1997), former music director of the Second Unitarian Church of Chicago.

117 O Light of Life
Emmon Bach (1929-) is professor emeritus of linguistics at the University of Massachusetts, Amherst.

META. Janet McLoud McGaughey (1914-2000), professor emeritus of music at the University of Texas at Austin, is the music director of the First Unitarian Universalist Church of Austin.

118 This Little Light of Mine
African American spiritual (ca. 1750-1875). In spite of the atrocities of slavery, African Americans developed a strong spiritual tradition that included dance, song, and religion.

LATTIMER. African American spiritual (ca. 1750-1875). This tune was named for Louis Lattimer (1848-1928), the son of a runaway slave, who worked on the electric light bulb with Thomas Edison, and with Alexander Graham Bell to create the drawings that helped secure the patent for the first telephone. Lattimer was a founding member of the Unitarian Church of Flushing, New York. This harmonization is by Horace Clarence Boyer. *See No. 30.*

119 Once to Every Soul and Nation
James Russell Lowell (1819-1891), a Unitarian, was a literary critic, poet, humorist, professor at Harvard University, and first editor of the *Atlantic Monthly*. He was US minister to Spain from 1877 to 1880 and to England from 1880 to 1885. His *Complete Poems* appeared in 1895. Stanzas from "The Present Crisis," protesting the war with Mexico, were first published by the English hymnologist W. Garrett Horder in *Hymns Supplemental*, 1896. Horder altered the text to make it regular enough to be sung.

EBENEZER. Thomas John Williams (1869-1944), native of Ynysmeudwy, Glamorganshire, Wales, was a pupil of David Evans (*see No. 38*) and organist and choirmaster at Llanelly. This tune was first published in *Llawlyfr Moliant (Handbook of Praise)*, 1890.

120 Turn Back
Clifford Bax (1886-1962), British dramatist and poet, was the younger brother of composer Arnold Bax. Bax wrote this hymn for the British composer Gustav Holst (*see No. 241*), who composed a motet on OLD 124TH, the tune that is generally associated with this text. In 1945 Bax stated that he was a Buddhist.
> OLD 124TH. This is the tune for Psalm 124 in the Genevan Psalter, 1543, and in the English and Scottish Psalters.

121 We'll Build a Land
These words from Isaiah and Amos were adapted by Barbara Zanotti (20th century), a peace activist now living in Maine.
> CREATION OF PEACE. Carolyn McDade (1935-), a feminist activist and songwriter, attends the Unitarian Universalist Community Church of Boston. This tune was arranged by Betsy Jo Angebranndt. *See No. 28.*

122 Sound Over All Waters
John Greenleaf Whittier. *See No. 9.* This text consists of stanzas from Whittier's "A Christmas Carmen," published in *Hazel-blossoms*, 1875, adapted by Arthur Foote II. *See No. 673.*
> ST. DENIO. Welsh ballad tune. Known in Wales as "Joanna," this tune is closely related to several other Welsh ballad tunes, notably "Can Mlynedd i 'nawr" ("A Hundred Years from Now"). It became a hymn tune, "Palestrina," in *Caniadau y Cyssegr*, Denbigh, North Wales, 1839, edited by John Roberts (Henllan) (1807-1876).

123 Spirit of Life
Carolyn McDade. *See No. 121.* This text was written as a prayer.
> SPIRIT OF LIFE. Carolyn McDade. *See No. 121.* Harmonization by Grace Lewis-McLaren. *See No. 73.*

124 Be That Guide
Carl G. Seaburg. *See No. 37.*
> WOODLAND. Thomas Benjamin. *See No. 2.*

125 From the Crush of Wealth and Power
Kendyl L. R. Gibbons. *See No. 51.* This text was commissioned for *Singing the Living Tradition.*
> BRIDEGROOM. Peter Cutts (1937-) is a composer and senior lecturer in music, Bretton Hall College of Higher Education, Wakefield, England. This is his most widely published tune.

126   Come, Thou Fount of Every Blessing

Robert Robinson (1735-1790), a minister, is the author of verse 1. Verses 2 and 3 are by Eugene B. Navias (1928-), a Unitarian Universalist minister of religious education who has served congregations in Cleveland, Ohio; Concord, New Hampshire; and Boston, Massachusetts. In 1963 he began working at the Unitarian Universalist Association in the religious education department and was its director from 1982 to 1992. He received the UUA's Angus H. MacLean Award for excellence in religious education in 1977.

> NETTLETON. John Wyeth. *See No. 53.* From his *Repository of Sacred Music*, Part II, 1813.

127   Can I See Another's Woe?

William Blake. *See No. 17.* This text is drawn from the first three stanzas of "On Another's Sorrow" in *Songs of Innocence.*

> NUN KOMM, DER HEIDEN HEILAND. Derived from the plainsong melody of its Latin original, "Veni Redemptor gentium," this tune was published with Martin Luther's translation in the *Erfurt Enchiridion*, 1524, and harmonized in 1594 by Seth Calvisius (1556-1615), a predecessor of Johann Hermann Schein (*see No. 183*) and Johann Sebastian Bach (*see No. 41*) as cantor of St. Thomas' School, Leipzig, Germany.

128   For All That Is Our Life

Bruce Findlow (1922-1994) was a British Unitarian minister. Born in Victoria, Australia, he discovered Unitarianism during World War II. In 1954, he moved to England to begin his theological studies at Oxford. He served congregations in Worcestershire and Edinburgh. From 1974 to 1985 he was principal of Manchester College, Oxford. His publications include *I Question Easter, Finding the Place*, and *Religion in People.*

> SHERMAN ISLAND. Patrick L. Rickey (1964-) is a composer and pianist from Oakland, California, who served for ten years as pianist and organist at Westminster Hill Presbyterian Church in Hayward, California. The tune is named for Sherman Island, California, where Rickey indulges one of his other passions, windsurfing.

129   Let Love Continue Long

Berkley L. Moore (1932-) is minister emeritus of the Abraham Lincoln Unitarian Universalist Congregation, Springfield, Illinois. This text expands on Hosea Ballou's famous phrase, which is reprinted as No. 705 of *Singing the Living Tradition.*

LOVE UNKNOWN. John Ireland (1879-1962) was an English composer, pianist, and teacher. Born in Bowdon, Cheshire, England, Ireland served as organist and choirmaster at St. Luke's, Chelsea, for twenty-two years and taught composition at the Royal College of Music for more than sixteen years. His compositions include *The Phantasie Trio*, 1906; *The Forgotten Rite*, 1913; *Cello Sonata*, 1923; *Piano Concerto*, 1930; and *Fantasy-Sonata*, 1943.

130   O Liberating Rose
Mark Belletini. *See No. 73.* These words were written for the dedication service of the Mark DeWolfe House, a home for people with AIDS supported by the University Unitarian Church in Seattle. The text is based on a conversation about "new kinds of theistic language" that the author had with Canadian Unitarian Universalist minister Mark DeWolfe (*see No. 295*) before his death from AIDS-related complications.

INITIALS. Larry Phillips. *See No. 37.* This tune was written in 1981 as a gift for his father's sixtieth birthday. The pitches in the original tune were selected through a formula using the initials of his father, his mother, and their five children, by relating these to the seven pitches in the Western tonal system.

131   Love Will Guide Us
Sally Rogers (20th century) is a veteran singer-songwriter whose works promote justice, unity, and peace. Her recordings for children include *What Can One Little Person Do?*, Round River Records, 1992, and *Piggyback Planet*, Round River Records, 1991.

OLYMPIA. Traditional tune arranged by Betty A. Wylder. *See No. 109.* This tune was named for Olympia Brown. *See No. 569.*

132   Bright Those Jewels
Hosea Ballou II (1796-1861), a Universalist minister, served congregations in Connecticut and Massachusetts. He edited many Universalist magazines and published his *Ancient History of Universalism* in 1829. He became the first president of Tufts College in 1852, after the Universalist denomination founded and incorporated the school.

ORIENTIS PARTIBUS. Medieval French melody harmonized by Richard Redhead (1820-1901), an English organist and composer. Redhead produced the first Anglican plainsong psalter, *Laudes Diurnae*, 1843, as well as other liturgical music for Anglo-Catholic use.

133   One World This
Vincent B. Silliman. *See No. 42.* This text was written for the 1947 fall conference of the American Unitarian Association.

SAVANNA. Dede Duson (1938-) is a music instructor, accompanist, and composer from Dallas, Texas. This tune was commissioned for *Singing the Living Tradition.*

134   Our World Is One World
Cecily Taylor (1930-) is a writer and poet. A collection of her poems, *Contact,* was published in 1972.

CHERNOBYL. Cecily Taylor. *See No. 133.* Arranged by Richard Graves (1926-).

135   How Happy Are They
Sir Henry Wotton (1568-1639), British author and public servant, was engaged for years in diplomatic missions in continental Europe and later served as provost of Eton. His writings, including this 1616 poem, were published in *Reliquiae Wottonianae* by Isaak Walton in 1651. Several phrases in this text are from Ben Jonson's copy of the poem; several stanzas are omitted and the text has been adapted.

WAREHAM. William Knapp. *See No. 92.*

136   Where Gentle Tides Go Rolling By
Richard Fariña (20th century) was a member of the editorial committee of *How Can I Keep From Singing!*, a songbook published by the First Unitarian Church of Los Angeles, California, in 1976.

ASIA. Traditional Asian melody harmonized by Betsy Jo Angebranndt. *See No. 28.*

137   We Utter Our Cry
Fred Kaan. *See No. 59.* This text was written for the opening service of the Christian World Conference on Life and Peace, 1983.

UPPSALA. Peter Cutts. *See No. 125.*

138   These Things Shall Be
John Addington Symonds (1840-1893) was a British critic and literary historian, student of Dante and the Greek poets, and author of the seven-volume *History of the Italian Renaissance,* 1875-1886. This text, from his *New and Old,* 1880, is part of the poem, "A Vista."

TRURO. Thomas Williams's *Psalmodia Evangelica. See No. 12.*

139   Wonders Still the World Shall Witness
Jacob Trapp (1899-1992), a Unitarian Universalist minister, served churches in Utah, Denver, and New Jersey. A prolific writer and poet, his books include *The Word to Jesus*, 1950; *Bhakti, Santi: Love Peace*, the 1971 Unitarian Universalist Meditation Manual; and *Return to the Springs*, 1987. He wrote this hymn in 1932 after a peace rally in Salt Lake City. A revised version was included in *Hymns of the Spirit*, 1937.

> IN BABILONE. From *Oude en nieuwe Hollantse Boernlities en Contradanseu* (Old and New Dutch Songs and Country Dances), ca. 1710.

140   Hail the Glorious Golden City
Felix Adler (1851-1933), German-born author and rabbi's son, was professor of social and political ethics at Columbia University. In 1876, he founded the New York Society for Ethical Culture and was thereafter the central figure in the American Ethical Culture movement. This text has been slightly revised by J. Hutton Hynd, ethical leader.

> HYFRYDOL. Welsh composer Rowland Hugh Prichard (1811-1887) wrote this tune around 1830, but it was first published by Griffith Roberts in *Haleliwiah Drachefn*, 1855. In the meantime, Prichard had published other original tunes in *Cyfaill y Cantorion*, 1844.

141   I've Got a New Name
African American spiritual (ca. 1750-1875).

> NEW NAME. African American spiritual (ca. 1750-1875), arranged by Wendell Whalum (1932-1987), a composer, arranger, choral conductor, and authority on gospel music.

142   Let There Be Light
Frances W. Davis (1936-1976) was a Canadian.

> CONCORD. Robert J. B. Fleming (1921-1976) was a Canadian composer whose work included film scores, piano music, ballets, and Canadian folk songs. Born in Prince Albert, Saskatchewan, Fleming served in the Royal Canadian Air Force, then joined the National Film Board as composer, conductor, and music editor. In 1970 he left the film industry and joined the music department of Carleton University, Ottawa.

143   Not in Vain the Distance Beacons
Alfred, Lord Tennyson. *See No. 58.* This text is arranged from "Locksley

Hall," 1842. An earlier version was published in *Hymns for the Celebration of Life*, 1964, as "The Parliament of Man."

    HYMN TO JOY. Ludwig van Beethoven. *See No. 29.*

144   Now Is the Time Approaching

Jane Laurie Borthwick (1813-1897), a Scottish hymn writer, edited and published several collections of hymns with her sister, Sarah Laurie Borthwick Findlater (1823-1907). This text, originally beginning "And is the time approaching," first appeared in *Thoughts for Thoughtful Hours*, 1859, as "Anticipations." Written as a vision of Christian unity, it is here recast as a hymn of world community.

    WEBB. George James Webb (1803-1887) wrote this as a secular song beginning, "'Tis dawn, the lark is singing," which was published in his *Odeon*, 1837. Born near Salisbury, England, Webb moved to Boston in 1830 and became organist of Old South Church. A close associate of Lowell Mason (*see No. 87*), he helped organize the Boston Academy of Music. He became a conductor and was president of the Handel and Haydn Society in 1840. In 1870 he followed Mason to New York.

145   As Tranquil Streams

Marion Franklin Ham. *See No. 13.* This text was written in 1933 and published in *Hymns of the Spirit*, 1937. It celebrates the growing closeness of the Unitarian and Universalist denominations for approximately a century, which culminated in their consolidation into the Unitarian Universalist Association in 1961.

    WINCHESTER NEW. This tune is adapted from a setting of "Wer nur den lieben Gott," in *Musicalisch Hand-buch der geistlichen Melodien*, printed not by Georg Wittwe, but by the widow of Georg Rebenlein, Hamburg, Germany, 1690. The Rebenlein family had been printers in Hamburg since around 1630.

146   Soon the Day Will Arrive

Ehud Manor (20th century) wrote the Hebrew original of this song, "Bashanah haba'a," which expresses belief in a better tomorrow.

    BASHANAH. Nurit Hirsch (20th century) is an Israeli composer.

147   When All the Peoples on This Earth

Anonymous.

    CHRISTMAS HYMN. Betsy Jo Angebranndt. *See No. 28.*

148   Let Freedom Span Both East and West

Jacob Trapp. *See No. 139.*

> MCKEE. African American spiritual (ca. 1750-1875) adapted and harmonized by Harry T. Burleigh (1866-1949), singer, composer, and arranger of spirituals. Born in Erie, Pennsylvania, he was quickly recognized as a talented singer. In 1894, he became soloist in the choir of St. George's Protestant Episcopal Church and in 1900 held the same post at the Temple Emmanuel. His arrangements of spirituals sparked the interest of many composers, including Antonin Dvorák.

149   Lift Every Voice and Sing

James Weldon Johnson (1871-1938), writer, attorney, and diplomat, served as US consul to Venezuela and Nicaragua. In 1930 he became professor of creative writing at Fisk University. He wrote numerous books of poetry and nonfiction and edited several pioneering anthologies of Black writing. This text is regarded by many to be the African American national anthem.

> LIFT EVERY VOICE. J. Rosamond Johnson (1873-1954), brother of James Weldon Johnson, spent seven years composing musicals and songs with his brother for use on the stage.

150   All Whose Boast It Is

James Russell Lowell. *See No. 119.* These are stanzas 1, 3, and 4 of his antislavery "Stanzas on Freedom," in *Poems*, 1844. This form was used first in a hymnbook in *A Book of Hymns*, 1846.

> SALZBURG. Jacob Hintze (1622-1702) was the court musician to the elector of Brandenburg at Berlin, Germany. This tune appears with the text "Alle Menschen müssen sterben" in *Praxis Pietatis Melica*, 1678, one of the editions edited by Hintze after Johann Crüger's death in 1662. This version is No. 153 of J. S. Bach's 371 chorale harmonizations. *See No. 41.*

151   I Wish I Knew How

Billy Taylor and Dick Dallas. Billy Taylor (1921-), jazz pianist, composer, arranger, and conductor began his musical career in New York's nightclubs, playing piano alongside some of the great performers in the bebop movement. He founded Jazzmobile, an outreach program that brings free music performances to people across the country.

> MANDELA. Billy Taylor and Dick Dallas, arranged by Mary Allen Walden. *See No. 116.* This tune is named in honor of Nelson Mandela (1918-) the first Black president of South Africa.

152 Follow the Drinking Gourd

Traditional African American spiritual (ca. 1750-1875). One of the best known of the "map songs" (*see No. 116*), which told runaway slaves to follow the Big Dipper to freedom. Similar songs have been lost because of their obvious use for covert communication, whereas spirituals whose religious content more thoroughly masked their intended message have survived.

> DRINKING GOURD. Traditional African American spiritual (ca. 1750-1875).

153 Oh, I Woke Up This Morning

African American spiritual (ca. 1750-1875).

> WATKINS HARPER. African American spiritual (ca. 1750-1875). This tune is named in honor of Frances Ellen Watkins Harper (1825-1911), a Unitarian author, lecturer, and social reformer born in Baltimore of free parents.

154 No More Auction Block for Me

African American spiritual. The peck of corn and pint of salt to which the text refers were slavery rations.

> AUCTION BLOCK. African American spiritual (ca. 1750-1875).

155 Circle 'Round for Freedom

Linda Hirschhorn (1947-) is a singer, songwriter, and cantorial soloist from Oakland, California.

> CIRCLE CHANT. Linda Hirschhorn (1947-).

156 Oh, Freedom

African American spiritual (ca. 1750-1875) sung in secret meetings of slaves for spiritual and psychological survival. The words express bondaged people's presumption that even though their bodies were not their own, their souls would never be enslaved. In some instances the singers were also expressing resistance. According to Arthur C. Jones (*see No. 99*) the words to this song were written around the "announcement of emancipation" and sung at African American gatherings in the 1880s, throughout the civil rights movements of the 1960s, and around the world in movements for freedom and justice.

> ROSA. African American spiritual (ca. 1750-1875) arranged by Horace Clarence Boyer. *See No. 30.* This tune is named in honor of Rosa Parks, a US civil rights activist, known as the mother of the civil rights movement.

157   Step by Step the Longest March
Early American labor poem.
> SOLIDARITY. Irish folk song adapted and arranged by Waldemar Hille.
> *See No. 9.*

158   Praise the Source of Faith and Learning
Thomas H. Troeger (1945-) is professor of preaching and communications at the Iliff School of Theology, Denver, Colorado. His numerous publications concern preaching and worship.
> PROCESSION. William Albright. *See No. 43.* This tune was commissioned by the First Unitarian Universalist Church of Ann Arbor, Michigan, for its 125th anniversary in 1990.

159   This Is My Song
Lloyd Stone (1912-) lives in Hawaii. This text was written as a prayer for peace.
> FINLANDIA. Jean Sibelius (1865-1957) was a dominant figure in the development of Finnish music. Born in Hämeenlinna, Sibelius was greatly influenced by the Finnish national epic *Kalevala*, Norse mythology, and nature poetry. He began composing and playing the violin at an early age, and his music for orchestra achieved great popularity in Finland and abroad. This tune, composed as the chorale for his famous symphonic poem, *Finlandia* (1900), became strongly associated with the patriotic movement to free Finland from Russia.

160   Far Too Long, by Fear Divided
John Andrew Storey. *See No. 2.*
> LOBT DEN HERRN, DIE MORGENSONNE. From *Allgemeines evangelisches Choralbuch*, 1829, edited by Johann Friedrich Naue (1787-1858), who was music director of the united universities of Halle and Wittenberg, Germany.

161   Peace! The Perfect Word Is Sounding
Odell Shepard (1884-1967) was an American writer and anthologist. His books include *The Joys of Forgetting*, 1928; *The Lore of the Unicorn*, 1930; and edited collections of work by Henry David Thoreau, Henry Wadsworth Longfellow, and others. In 1933 he won the Pulitzer Prize for Biography for *Pedlar's Progress*, a life of Bronson Alcott.
> CHARLESTON. From William Walker's *The Southern Harmony*. *See No. 15.* Harmonization by Alastair Cassels-Brown (1927-).

162   Gonna Lay Down My Sword and Shield
African American Spiritual (ca. 1750-1875).
> DOWN BY THE RIVERSIDE. African American spiritual (ca. 1750-1875)
> arranged by Mary Allen Walden. *See No. 116.*

163   For the Earth Forever Turning
Kim Oler (20th century) wrote this hymn for Paul Winter's "Missa Gaia"
("Earth Mass"), recorded live in the Cathedral of St. John the Divine and
the Grand Canyon in 1981. The text was suggested by Paul Winter, who
was inspired by the story of Physling, the blind poet on the Venus Shuttle
in Robert Heinlein's science fiction classic, *The Green Hills of Earth.*
Physling wrote a ballad yearning for "one more landing on the globe that
gave us birth," and his last lyric was, "May we rest our eyes on the fleecy
skies and the cool green hills of earth." Oler shaped this inspiration into
verse to complete this lyrical hymn.
> BLUE-GREEN HILLS OF EARTH. Kim Oler (20th century). This arrangement
> is by Nick Page (1952-) and Jim Scott (1946-), Unitarian Univer-
> salist songwriters.

164   The Peace Not Past Our Understanding
John Holmes. *See No. 11.*
> SURSUM CORDA. Alfred Morton Smith. *See No. 54.*

165   When Windows That Are Black and Cold
Rachel Bates (20th century), British author and poet.
> DANBY. English melody, adapted and harmonized by Ralph Vaughan
> Williams. *See No. 17.*

166   Years Are Coming
Adin Ballou (1803-1890) was a Universalist minister who founded the
Hopedale Community, an experiment in "practical Christianity," in 1842.
In 1849 *The Hopedale Collection of Hymns and Songs for the Use of Practical Christians*, compiled by Ballou and containing twenty of his pieces,
was issued. This text, titled "Reign of Christian Peace" and credited to
Hopedale College, is included in *The Gospel Psalmist*, 1861, in the section
on "Christian Philanthropy and Reform." Two syllables were added to line
4 of each quatrain.
> HYFRYDOL. Rowland Hugh Prichard. *See No. 140.*

167   Nothing but Peace Is Enough

Jim Scott (1946-) is a Unitarian Universalist singer-songwriter who has performed with the Paul Winter Consort. He lives in Eugene, Oregon.

> NOTHING BUT PEACE. Jim Scott (1946-).

168   One More Step

Joyce Poley (1941-), a singer and songwriter, attends the Beacon Unitarian Church in Coquitlam, British Columbia. This hymn was written in 1986 for a worship service packet sponsored and distributed by the Unitarian Universalist Peace Network.

> ONE MORE STEP. Joyce Poley (1941-). This harmonization is by Grace Lewis-McLaren. *See No. 73.*

169   We Shall Overcome

African American spiritual (ca. 1750-1875). During the civil rights movement the words to many African American spirituals were changed to indicate unity. "I Shall Overcome" became "We Shall Overcome." In spirituals, however, "I" is not used to signify one person but means everyone who has been oppressed and who sings the song.

> MARTIN. African American spiritual (ca. 1750-1875), adapted by William Farley Smith (1941-), minister of music at Harlem's St. Mark's United Methodist Church in New York. He founded the Harlem Multi-ethnic Choral Symposium and served as a consultant, editor, and arranger for the 1989 *United Methodist Hymnal.* The tune is named for Martin Luther King, Jr. *See No. 584.*

170   We Are a Gentle, Angry People

Holly Near (1949-) is a singer and songwriter. Born in Ukiah, California, she has performed on stage since she was seven years old, and recorded her first song before she reached her teens. In 1973 she formed the Redwood Records Company. Her autobiography, *Fire in the Rain . . . Singer in the Storm,* was published in 1990. This song was written in response to the 1978 murder of Harvey Milk, a gay member of the San Francisco city council, and was recorded under the title "Singing for Our Lives."

> SINGING FOR OUR LIVES. Holly Near (1949-). This arrangement is by Patrick L. Rickey. *See No. 128.*

171   N'kosi Sikelel' i Afrika

Enoch Mankayi Sontongo (1860-1904), a Christian singer and songwriter, wrote this song in 1897. First performed in 1899, this song rapidly spread throughout churches and schools in South Africa, partly because it was sung in concerts by the Ohlange Zulu Choir, and was adopted by the African National Congress and other organizations as a national hymn. Despite being banned by the South African government, the song was sung at meetings, rallies, funerals, and other public gatherings. Since the fall of apartheid, it has become one of the two official national anthems of South Africa.

AFRIKA. Enoch Sontongo (1860-1904).

172   Siph' Amandla
South African freedom song from the era of apartheid. This song is included in *Freedom Is Coming: Songs of Protest and Praise from South Africa,* collected and edited by Anders Nyberg, 1984.

TUTU. South African tune, named in honor of Desmond Tutu. *See No. 593.*

173   In the Branches of the Forest
David Arkin (20th century) was a member of the committee that created *How Can We Keep From Singing!*, 1976, published by the First Unitarian Church of Los Angeles, California.

MOUNTAIN ALONE. Waldemar Hille. *See No. 9.*

174   O, Earth You Are Surpassing Fair
John Andrew Storey. *See No. 2.*

MERTHYR TYDFIL. Joseph Parry (1841-1903) was a Welsh composer who rose to almost legendary standing among Welsh musicians. From Merthyr Tydfil, his family emigrated to Pennsylvania when Parry was thirteen. He traveled between Wales and the United States composing and studying and eventually earned enough money to attend the Royal Academy of Music, London. He received a bachelor's degree and a doctorate in music at Cambridge, established a music school in Swansea, and directed music at the University of Wales and the University College of South Wales and Monmouthshire in Cardiff. Parry composed the first Welsh opera, *Blowden,* 1878.

175   We Celebrate the Web of Life
Alicia S. Carpenter. *See No. 6.* This text was commissioned for *Singing the Living Tradition.*

CHRISTUS DER IST MEIN LEBEN. Melchior Vulpius (ca. 1560-1616), cantor at Weimar, Germany, composer of chorale melodies and more elaborate choral works, published this tune in *Schön geistlich Gesangbuch,* 1609.

176   Daya Kar Daan Bhakti Ka
Hindu Prayer, translated as follows:
Refrain: Please bestow upon us, O Supreme Soul, the gift of devotion.
               Please bestow upon our souls (the gift of) purity.
Stanza 1:   Come in our meditation, O God, reside in our eyes.
               Come into our dark hearts, arouse the Supreme Light.
Stanza 2:   Flow the river (Ganges) of love in the hearts, O Ocean of Love,
               Teach us, O God, to live together in harmony.
Stanza 3:   Let service be our creed, let service be our action,
               Make us earnest servers whose service is ever honest.
INDIAN PRAYER. Traditional Indian, arranged by Sanjeev Ramabhadran
(1975-), a student of Indian classical music under the tutelage of
Sri Ran Phatak, a composer in India.

177   Cherry Blooms
Japanese folk song with English words by Edwin Markham (1852-1940),
who began his career as a teacher, principal, and superintendent in California schools. In 1899 he published *The Man with the Hoe and Other Poems*
and moved to New York City to write. *Lincoln and Other Poems* followed
in 1901, and other collections of poetry appeared until the final volume,
The Star of Araby, 1937. William Wolff (1909-), musicologist, songwriter,
and song collector, provided the alternate text to commemorate Hiroshima
Day.
SAKURA. Japanese folk song.

178   Raghupati
Traditional Hindu text. According to Hindu mythology, Ram is one of
twelve incarnations of God. The first verse calls to Ram by several of his
names and titles. The second verse says, "Oh God, please give good coun-
sel to us who may call you Eeswar and us who may call you Allah, and lead
us properly." Mohandas Gandhi loved this song, which calls for peace between Moslem and Hindu.
RAM. Traditional Hindu tune.

179   Words That We Hold Tight
Bishop Dr. Adedeji Ishola (20th century) founded the Unitarian Brother-
hood Church of Lagos, Nigeria, in 1919 as an indigenous African initia-
tive. It was the first African church to introduce African cultural elements
into its liturgy and to baptize its children with names in the native Yoruba
language. His Yoruba text has been translated and adapted.
EKO A BA KO. Traditional Yoruba tune.

180   Alhamdulillah
William Allaudin Mathieu (1937-) is a composer, performer, author, and teacher. The Alhamdulillah Round was written in 1970 under the guidance of Sufi master Samuel Lewis. Mathieu began to compose prayers for group music practice to express his understanding of how all humanity prays one prayer and sings one song.

MATHIEU. William Allaudin Mathieu (1937-).

181   No Matter If You Live Now Far or Near
Sutta Nopata.

INDIA. Old Indian song, harmonized by Frédéric Mathil in 1950.

182   O, the Beauty in a Life
Bishop Toribio S. Quimada was an ordained minister of the Universal Church of Christ when he was introduced to the teachings of the Universalist Church of America. He subsequently founded the Universalist (now Unitarian Universalist) Church of the Philippines, which affiliated with the Universalist Church of America in 1954. This text has been shortened and adapted.

QUIMADA. Traditional Visayan (Filipino) folk tune.

183   The Wind of Change Forever Blown
Sarojini Naidu (1879-1949), Indian poet and reformer, became the first woman president of the Indian National Congress in 1925. Her three books of poetry—*The Golden Threshold*, *The Bird of Time*, and *The Broken Wing*—have been widely translated.

MACH'S MIT MIR, GOTT. Johann Hermann Schein (1586-1630), a predecessor of Johann Sebastian Bach (*see No. 41*) as cantor of St. Thomas' School, Leipzig, Germany, composed this tune and issued it in 1628 as a memorial tribute. This version is No. 44 of Bach's 371 chorale harmonizations.

184   Be Ye Lamps unto Yourselves
Gautama Buddha (5th century BCE). This beloved Buddhist text is from "Buddha's Farewell Address," which, like all texts attributed to the Buddha, was not committed to writing until centuries after his death. This passage from the Mahaparinibbana Suttanta, however, is believed to strike an authentic note. This anonymous translation resembles that of C. Rhys Davids from the Pali in *Sacred Books of the Buddhists*, Vol. III, Part 3.

LUMINA. From the plainsong setting of "Splendor paternae gloriae," in the *Sarum Antiphonal*, used in the liturgy of Salisbury Cathedral before the Reformation.

185   Your Mercy, Oh Eternal One
Rabindranath Tagore (Ravindranatha Thakura) (1861-1941) was a prolific Bengali poet and philosopher who was awarded the Nobel Prize for Literature in 1913. His books include *Binodini*, a novel, 1902; *Gitanjali*, a book of poetry based on medieval Indian devotional lyrics, 1912; and *Chitra*, a play, 1914. He was active in educational and social reform in India and was knighted in 1915, but he renounced the honor in 1919 to protest British repression. He was also a gifted composer and painter, and his song "Our Golden Bengal" became the national anthem of Bangladesh.

DUNDEE, the English title, is called "French tune" in the Scottish Psalter of 1615, where it is one of the twelve common tunes. This tune was harmonized by Thomas Ravenscroft (1592-1635), British composer, editor, and arranger, who was trained in the choir of St. Paul's Cathedral and Cambridge. Collections of music he edited include *Pammelia*, 1609, and *Deuteromelia*, 1609.

186   Grieve Not Your Heart
Confucius (551-479 BCE) was a Chinese teacher, philosopher, and political theorist who lived in an era of political violence and social disintegration. He believed that thoughts and actions could restore society, and adopted teachings based on "human heartedness" (sympathy), benevolence, and virtue. After the philosopher's death, Confucianism became the state religion of China and remained so until the late twentieth century, a source of values and social code for Taoists, Buddhists, and Christians in many parts of Asia. These lines, reminiscent of *The Analects* 1:16, 4:17, 12:16, and 15:23, were recast by John Andrew Storey. *See No. 2.*

PRIMROSE. From *Kentucky Harmony*, 1816.

187   It Sounds Along the Ages
William Channing Gannett. *See No. 39.* The original four stanzas constitute the hymn "The Word of God," found in *Unity Hymns and Chorals*, revised, 1911. Stanzas 1 and 2, with a new stanza 3 made from the original 3 and 4, appeared in *Hymns of the Spirit*, 1937. Stanza 3 appears in this form in *We Sing of Life*, 1955.

FAR OFF LANDS. The Bohemian Brethren created this melody. It is named by its association with "Remember all the people," written for children by Percy Dearmer in 1929. Swedish Lutherans in the

United States were familiar with the tune, which the Augustana Synod published in *Hemlandssånger*, 1892, with the text "Du ömma fadershjerta." This version was arranged.

188   Come, Come Whoever You Are
Jalal al-Din Rumi, Maulana (1207-1273), Sufi poet, was born in Afghanistan into a long line of scholars, jurists, and theologians. When he was thirty-seven he met a wandering holy man, Shams al-Din of Tabriz. With Shams he discovered the inner Friend, the soul, the Beloved, a constant reminder of God's presence. He subsequently wrote some 30,000 verses as well as the epic *Masnavi-ye Ma'navi*. This text has been adapted.

> PILGRIMAGE. Lynn Adair Ungar (1963-) is a Unitarian Universalist minister serving the Second Unitarian Church in Chicago, Illinois. Previously, she served the Unitarian Universalist Church of the Palouse in Moscow, Idaho. She is the author of the 1996 UUA Meditation Manual, *Blessing the Bread*.

189   Light of Ages and of Nations
Samuel Longfellow. *See No. 12.* Written in 1860, this hymn first appeared in *Hymns of the Spirit*, 1864, with the opening line, "God of ages." This hymn was one of the first to fully recognize non-Christian religious traditions.

> IN BABILONE. *See No. 139.*

190   Light of Ages and of Nations
Samuel Longfellow. *See No. 12.*

> AUSTRIA. Franz Joseph Haydn. *See No. 81.* Haydn wrote this melody as part of a string quartet he composed in 1799. Because the tune was used during the Nazi regime as the German national anthem, we offer IN BABILONE (No. 189) as an alternate. We have retained AUSTRIA to signal that Nazism has not had the final victory by ruining this fine melody of Haydn.

191   Now I Recall My Childhood
Rabindranath Tagore. *See No. 185.* This text was adapted by Kenneth L. Patton *(see No. 303)* from poem 71 in *Crossing*.

> SURSUM CORDA. Alfred Morton Smith. *See No. 54.*

192   Nay, Do Not Grieve
Sarojini Naidu. *See No. 183.* This poem appeared in Naidu's *The Bird of Time*, 1912.

NAIDU. Libby Larsen. *See No. 80.* This tune was commissioned for *Singing the Living Tradition.*

193 Our Faith Is but a Single Gem
John Andrew Storey. *See No. 2.*
> DISTRESS. From William Walker's *The Southern Harmony*, 1835. *See No. 15.*

194 Faith Is a Forest
Shelley Jackson Denham. *See No. 55.* This piece was commissioned for *Singing the Living Tradition.*
> MO-LI-HUA. A Chinese folk melody that depicts the beauty of the jasmine flower, adapted by I-to Loh. *See No. 24.*

195 Let Us Wander Where We Will
Robert Louis Stevenson (1850-1894) was a Scottish novelist, essayist, and poet. Leisurely travels in France by canoe and on foot, passage in the steerage of an immigrant ship to America, traveling across America in an immigrant train, and his final years in Samoa provided material for such books as *Treasure Island, Kidnapped*, and *A Child's Garden of Verses*. This text is from the poem "Swallows Travel To and Fro," written in 1873, and published in *Poems by Robert Louis Stevenson Hitherto Unpublished*, 1916.
> TOA-SIA. Traditional Taiwanese melody, adapted from a traditional tribal melody from Taiwan; now considered a real Taiwanese hymn. Harmonized by I-to Loh. *See No. 24.*

196 Singer of Life
Texcoco Nahuatl poem. Arranging flowers was an Aztec art form, and Aztec poems often linked the image of fragile flowers to the concept of mortality.
> LACQUIPARLE. Native American melody, harmonized by Richard Proulx (1937-), a composer, conductor, and organist. Born in St. Paul, Minnesota, Proulx has served several churches as music director, including the St. Thomas Episcopal Church in Seattle. He has published several compositions for chorus and for organ.

197 There Are Numerous Strings
Rabindranath Tagore. *See No. 185.* This text is poem 68 in *Crossing*.
> TAGORE. Rabindranath Tagore's tune was harmonized by Betsy Jo Angebranndt. *See No. 28.*

198   God of Many Names
Brian Wren. *See No. 23.*

> MANY NAMES. William P. Rowan (1951-) is a composer, organist, and director of music at St. Mary Cathedral, Lansing, Michigan. This tune was first written for a 1985 American Guild of Organists hymn contest.

199   Precious Lord, Take My Hand
Thomas A. Dorsey (1899-1993), born in Villa Rica, Georgia, is known to many as the father of gospel music. This blues singer, gospel songwriter, and pianist was greatly influenced by blues pianists in Atlanta. In 1923 he formed his own band, the Wildcat's Jazz Band, with whom Ma Rainey performed. For forty years, Dorsey was the choir director at Pilgrim Baptist Church, Chicago. His 1928 album, "Tight Like That" was a best-selling blues record. He wrote this text following the death of his wife.

> PRECIOUS LORD. Thomas A. Dorsey (1899-1993).

200   A Mighty Fortress
Martin Luther (1483-1546), German theologian, was the leader of the Protestant Reformation. His translation of the Bible has a classic quality for the German language comparable to that of the King James Version for English. A hymn writer and musician, he was primarily responsible for the importance of congregational song in Protestant churches. Thomas Carlyle said that this "Battle Hymn of the Reformation," based on Psalm 46, was "like the sound of Alpine avalanches, or the first murmur of earthquakes." This translation by Frederick Henry Hedge (*see No. 33*) has been used widely in North American Protestant churches.

> EIN' FESTE BURG. Martin Luther (1483-1546) is believed to be the author of this tune, first published in Joseph Klug's *Geistliche Lieder*, 1529. The harmony is by Johann Sebastian Bach. *See No. 41.*

201   Glory, Glory, Hallelujah!
Traditional.

> SOJOURNER. Traditional, arranged by Mary Allen Walden. *See No. 116.* The tune is named for Sojourner Truth (1797?-1883), the African American evangelist, abolitionist, reformer, and women's rights activist.

202   Come Sunday
Duke Ellington (1899-1974), one of the greatest jazz musicians of all time, was born in Washington, DC. This bandleader, composer, and pianist made

his professional debut at seventeen and played in clubs on Broadway, in Harlem, and in concerts at Carnegie Hall. He toured Europe and the former Soviet Union and in 1969 received the Presidential Medal of Honor. Ellington was the first jazz musician member of the Royal Music Academy in Stockholm. Though widely known for his "Jungle Style" music, he also wrote sacred music in his later years. This text, written during this time, commemorates Sunday as an important day in the Christian weekly calendar, signifying the resurrection of Jesus.

ELLINGTON. Duke Ellington (1899-1974).

203 All Creatures of the Earth and Sky

St. Francis of Assisi (1182-1226). Following a serious illness, Francis embarked c. 1206 on a life of ascetic devotion, preaching and ministering to the neglected. He founded the Franciscan order of friars in 1210. His joyousness and love of nature are reflected in this text, reputedly composed by him in the Umbrian dialect in his last year, making him among the first to adapt the Provençal troubadour style to religious use and to the Italian language. This is a fresh translation from the Italian.

LASST UNS ERFREUEN. From *Ausserlesene Catholische Geistliche Kirchgesäng*, printed by Peter von Brachel in Cologne, Germany, 1623. The tune bears a strong resemblance to the Genevan tune used for Psalms 36 and 68 (*Strassburger Kirchenamt*, 1525), which in England became "Old 113th." It was thus adapted and harmonized by Ralph Vaughan Williams. *See No. 17.*

204 Come, O Sabbath Day

Gustav Gottheil (1827-1903), a rabbi and leader of US Reform Judaism, was born in Prussian Posen, schooled in Berlin, and served briefly in Manchester, England. In 1873 he came to New York to serve as the rabbi of Temple Emanu-El until 1899. In 1887, he published *Hymns and Anthems Adapted for Jewish Worship*, one of the first Jewish hymnbooks printed in the United States, and the basis for successive editions of the *Union Hymnal*. He was a founder of the New York State Conference of Religions and helped establish the Jewish Publication Society of America.

SABBATH. Abraham W. Binder (1895-1966), a music director and composer, was born and lived in New York, New York. In 1918, he became the director of the School of Music at the Young Men's Hebrew Association of New York and he conducted the Jewish Choral Society until one year before his death. He edited several hymnbooks, including *The Union Hymnal*, 3rd edition, 1932.

205   Amazing Grace!

John Newton (1725-1807) was a slave trader who converted to Christianity under the influence of evangelist George Whitefield and the Wesley family. Ordained into the evangelical movement of the Church of England, he became an outspoken opponent of slavery.

> AMAZING GRACE. From *Columbian Harmony*, 1829, harmonized by Austin Cole Lovelace (1919-), an author, composer, and hymnbook editor. He has taught at Union Theological Seminary in New York; Garrett Seminary in Evanston, Illinois; Queens and Davidson Colleges in North Carolina; the University of Nebraska; and Iliff School of Theology in Denver, Colorado.

206   Amazing Grace!

John Newton. *See No. 205.*

> AMAZING GRACE. *See No. 205.* The arrangement and accompaniment are by J. Jefferson Cleveland (1937-1986), co-editor of the Methodist hymnal *Songs of Zion*, 1981.

207   Earth Was Given as a Garden

Roberta Bard (1940-) is a Unitarian Universalist Quaker and an active member of Lake Forest Friends Meeting and the Unitarian Church of Evanston, Illinois. Her lyrics reflect her concern for gender-inclusive and spiritually inclusive language. This hymn, written in 1989, was one of the winners in the Hymnbook Resources Commission's competition for hymn texts celebrating the feminine imagery of the divine.

> HYFRYDOL. Rowland Hugh Prichard. *See No. 140.*

208   Every Time I Feel the Spirit

African American spiritual (ca. 1750-1875).

> PENTECOST. African American spiritual (ca. 1750-1875), adapted and arranged by William Farley Smith. *See No. 169.*

209   O Come, You Longing Thirsty Souls

A metrical adaptation of Isaiah 55:1-2, 10-13, a beautiful text written in Hebrew ca. 540 BCE by an anonymous prophet and poet now called Second Isaiah or deutero-Isaiah. The author wrote to Judean exiles in captivity, comforting them and telling them that Yahweh had not abandoned them, despite their trouble.

> FOREST GREEN. English melody; harmony by Ralph Vaughan Williams. *See No. 17.*

210 Wade in the Water

African American spiritual (ca. 1750-1875). Like many "map songs" (*see No. 116*), this spiritual employed biblical themes to disguise instructions for escape. "Wade in the Water" was sung at baptisms, but Harriet Tubman also used it to warn escapees to wade in the water to throw off dogs and trackers.

> MCCREE. African American spiritual (ca. 1750-1875) arranged by Mary Allen Walden. *See No. 116.* This tune was named in honor of Wade H. McCree, Jr. (1920-1987), the first African American to serve as United States Assistant Solicitor General and a vice moderator of the Unitarian Universalist Association from 1965 to 1966.

211 We Are Climbing Jacob's Ladder

African American spiritual (ca. 1750-1875). This song is believed to have been composed ca. 1824-1825 by Liberian and other slaves who intended to return to Africa once they were free. This song portrays the power of the spirit in the face of continuous sorrow and trials.

> JACOB'S LADDER. African American spiritual (ca. 1750-1875).

212 We Are Dancing Sarah's Circle

Carole A. Eagleheart (1944-), writer, composer, and performing artist, attends the Champlain Valley Unitarian Universalist Society in Middlebury, Vermont. This text was inspired by feminist theologian Nelle Morton.

> JACOB'S LADDER. African American spiritual (ca. 1750-1875).

213 There's a Wideness in Your Mercy

Frederick William Faber (1814-1863), an Anglican who converted to Roman Catholicism, helped found a community called Brothers of the Will of God, which later joined the Oratory of St. Philip Neri. Author of many theological books, Faber is best known for his 150 hymns. Here are stanzas 1, 5, and 4 of the original six; the text has been further adapted.

> CHARLESTON. From Amos Pilsbury's *United States' Sacred Harmony*, 1799.

214 Shabbat Shalom

Traditional Hebrew. The text, which translates as "Sabbath peace," is the customary greeting for Jews on the Sabbath.

> SHABBAT SHALOM. Traditional Hebrew arranged by S. Secunda (1894-1974).

215　Praise to the Living God

This text, originally named "The Yigdal" for its first Hebrew word, is sung antiphonally by cantor and congregation at the close of Jewish worship on the eve of the Sabbath and other festivals. Probably written by Daniel ben Judah Dayyan between 1396 and 1404, it is a versification of the thirteen articles of Jewish faith drawn up by Maimonides (1130-1205). A Christian hymn based on "The Yigdal," written ca. 1770 by Thomas Olivers, an English Methodist preacher, was used in England and the United States. In the 1880s Rabbi Max Landsberg of Temple Berith Kodesh in Rochester, New York, asked Newton Mann, minister of the Unitarian church there, to make a more exact translation. Later, Rabbi Landsberg asked Mann's successor, William Channing Gannett (*see No. 39*), to recast Mann's version in traditional meter. That version, omitting one stanza, appears here in revised form.

> LEONI. Synagogue melody. This tune is named for Meyer Lyon (1751-1797), cantor at the Great Synagogue, London, who transcribed and adapted it for Thomas Olivers. It is one of seven traditional tunes for the Yigdal and has been the accepted Friday evening tune in England for two centuries.

216　Hashiveinu

Traditional Hebrew. In translation, the text reads, "Turn us toward You, and we will return. Renew our days as of old."

> HASHIVEINU. Traditional Hebrew.

217　O Sing Hallelujah

Adapted from Psalm 150 and Avinu Malkeinu, a traditional Hebrew hymn for Rosh Hashanah (the Jewish New Year).

> SING HALLELUJAH. Abraham W. Binder. *See No. 204.*

218　Who Can Say

Adapted from *Gates of Repentance: The New Union Prayerbook for the Days of Awe*, edited by Chaim Stern, 1984. The text is an English translation of the Hebrew Prayer "Yih´yu l´ratzon," which is said at the end of the silent prayer portion of the service.

> A NEW HEART. Max Janowski (1912-1991) published more than 150 works, including liturgical pieces, folk songs, piano and organ solos, cantatas, and orchestral and chamber works.

219   O Hear, My People
Rabbi Nachman of Bratzlav (1770-1811).
> HEAR, MY PEOPLE. Leon Leopold Lewandowski (ca. 1821-ca. 1894) was a Polish violinist, composer, and bandmaster. Born in Kalisz, the son of Jewish intellectuals, Lewandowski organized his own orchestra and performed throughout Warsaw. He was best known for his dance genres, many of which he composed, yet also wrote music for orchestra, chorus, and instrumental ensembles.

220   Bring Out the Festal Bread
Mark L. Belletini. *See No. 73.*
> GILU HAGALILIM. Hebrew folk song.

221   Light One Candle
Peter Yarrow (1938-), folksinger and composer, is a member of the singing group Peter, Paul, and Mary.
> MACCABEE. Peter Yarrow's tune has been arranged by Betty A. Wylder. *See No. 109.*

222   Mi Y'Malel
Hebrew folk song.
> MI Y'MALEL. Hebrew folk song.

223   Rock of Ages, Let Our Song
Leopold Stein (1810-1882) was a scholar, liturgist, poet, dramatist, leader in Reform Judaism, and rabbi in Frankfurt-am-Main, Germany, for eighteen years. He wrote the German original of this text to replace a thirteenth- or fourteenth-century Hebrew text, which also had an initial reference to a rock. This English adaptation is by Marcus Mordecai Jastrow (1829-1903) and Gustav Gottheil. *See No. 204.* Jastrow, born in Prussian Poland, educated in Germany and briefly a rabbi in Warsaw, was expelled from Poland for sympathizing with nationalistic rebels. He was a rabbi in Philadelphia from 1866 on. A scholar, liturgist, and teacher, until 1903 he was editor-in-chief of a translation of the Jewish scriptures into English that was published in 1917. Stanza 3, line 1, has been altered from "Children of the Martyr-race" to emphasize the prophetic role of Judaism. Hanukkah, a Jewish festival involving the lighting of one to eight candles on successive nights, commemorates the rededication of the Temple at Jerusalem in 165 BCE.

MOOZ TSUR. Based on German folk song phraseology. Used in the synagogue with the Hebrew text "Mooz Tsur," the tune is also sung by Jewish congregations with German and English texts.

224 Let Christmas Come

John Hanly Morgan (1918-) is a Unitarian Universalist minister. Born in New Albany, Indiana, Morgan served many congregations including the First Unitarian Congregation of Toronto, Ontario, where he is now minister emeritus.

DANBY. English melody, adapted and harmonized by Ralph Vaughan Williams. *See No. 17.*

225 O Come, O Come, Emmanuel

The Latin hymn may date to the ninth century or earlier. John Mason Neale (1818-1866), a noted hymnologist who rendered many early Christian hymns into English, created an English version from seven great antiphons saluting the Messiah with many symbolic names. This version has been extensively recast in order to emphasize the hymn's mystical imagery, rather than the ancient Christian image of the church as the New Israel.

VENI EMMANUEL. Thomas Helmore (1811-1890), musical editor of *The Hymnal Noted*, 1854, provided this tune for Neale's translation of the Latin hymn. The plainsong source is a fifteenth-century Franciscan processional. This tune was harmonized by John Weaver (1937-), a composer who is also organist and music director at Madison Avenue Presbyterian Church in New York City, as well as chair of the Organ Department at the Julliard School.

226 People, Look East

Eleanor Farjeon. *See No. 38.* This Advent carol was written for *The Oxford Book of Carols*, 1928.

BESANÇON. Traditional carol melody from Besançon in eastern France. This tune was harmonized by Martin Shaw (1875-1958).

227 Crèche Flickers Bright Here

Howard Box. *See No. 56.* This text was written to accompany a traditional Hungarian Christmas carol. The words allude to the Hungarian custom of caroling in the streets with lighted crèches called "Bethlehems."

MENNYBOL. Traditional Hungarian folk song arranged by Thomas Legrady, composer, conductor, and accompanist from Willowdale, Ontario. Legrady is a refugee from the 1958 Hungarian uprising.

228   Once in Royal David's City

Carl G. Seaburg. *See No. 37.* This hymn is based on a text of Mrs. C. F. Alexander.

IRBY. Henry John Gauntlett (1805-1876), an English organist, composer, and critic, was born in Wellington, Salop. Gauntlett compiled hymnbooks and is said to have boasted of composing 10,000 English hymn tunes. This harmonization is by Arthur Henry Mann (1850-1929), an English organist and choir director. Born in Norwich, England, Mann served as King's College's choirmaster for fifty-three years, during which time he took the choir from one of the worst in Cambridge to the most famous Anglican choir in the world. Mann also composed sacred choral music and hymn tunes.

229   Gather 'Round the Manger

Heather Lynn Hanson (1938-) is a Unitarian Universalist minister who has served congregations in Bellingham and Eugene, Washington, and Houston, Texas. Before entering the ministry, she served as choir director for the Michael Servetus Unitarian Universalist Fellowship in Vancouver, Washington. This hymn was written in 1986 as a Christmas gift for the children and members of that fellowship.

LOVE'S GIFT. Heather Lynn Hanson (1938-).

230   Duermete, Niño Lindo

Hispanic folk song, translated by John Donald Robb (1892-1989). In this text, Mary sings a lullaby to the infant Jesus. The text has been altered.

A LA RU. Hispanic folk song, arranged by John Donald Robb (1892-1989).

231   Angels We Have Heard on High

This French carol, with the text "Les anges dans nos campagnes" and its tune, "Gloria," were published in *Nouveau Recueil de Cantiques*, 1855. This English version, based on an anonymous translation, is by Earl Bowman Marlatt (1892-1976). A Methodist minister, Marlatt was a professor at Wellesley College, Boston University (where he served as dean of the School of Theology for seven years), and the Perkins Theological School of Southern Methodist University.

GLORIA. French carol. This tune was published in *Nouveau Recueil de Cantiques*, 1855.

232   The Hills Are Bare at Bethlehem
Royce J. Scherf (1929-).
> PROSPECT. From William Walker's *The Southern Harmony*, 1835. *See No. 15*. Harmonized by Thomas Somerville in 1969.

233   Bring a Torch, Jeannette, Isabella
Traditional Provençal hymn (17th century).
> BRING A TORCH. French carol. Traditional Provençal (17th century). The torches, or candles, of the ancient Jewish Festival of Lights (Hanukkah) played an important part in the Christmas celebrations of Provence and southern Europe. This carol is a beautiful example of the torch songs of that period.

234   In the Gentle of the Moon
Carl G. Seaburg. *See No. 37*.
> HASIDIM. *See No. 62*.

235   Deck the Hall with Boughs of Holly
Traditional Welsh carol.
> YULE. Old Welsh carol.

236   O Thou Joyful Day
Latin hymn (16th century).
> SICILIAN MARINERS. Folk song of the Sicilian seas first published in *The European Magazine and London Review*, 1792. This tune has been altered.

237   The First Nowell
English carol of unknown origin found in Davis Gilbert's *Ancient Christmas Carols*, 1823, and William Sandys's *Christmas Carols Ancient and Modern*, 1833. The words are not scripturally accurate, for the shepherds saw no star. The carol presumably dates from the seventeenth century or before.
> THE FIRST NOWELL. From Sandys's *Christmas Carols Ancient and Modern*. The harmonization, by Sir John Stainer (1840-1901), is from *Christmas Carols New and Old*, 1871.

238   Within the Shining of a Star
Robert S. Lehman (1913-), born in Cincinnati, Ohio, is a retired Unitarian Universalist minister. He served the First Unitarian Church in Minneapo-

lis, Minnesota, the First Unitarian Church in San Jose, California, and several other congregations.

CHRISTMAS HYMN. Betsy Jo Angebranndt. *See No. 28.*

239   Go Tell It on the Mountain

African American spiritual (ca. 1750-1875).

GO TELL IT ON THE MOUNTAIN. African American spiritual (ca. 1750-1875), arranged by Paul Sjolund (1935-).

240   I Heard the Bells on Christmas Day

Henry Wadsworth Longfellow (1807-1882), Unitarian and popular American poet, was commemorated by a bust in Westminster Abbey. Professor of Modern Languages at Bowdoin and Harvard Colleges, he resigned in 1854 to write. His works *Evangeline, Hiawatha*, and "Paul Revere's Ride" are among his best known. In hymn writing he was outshone by his brother, Samuel, of whom he said, "I am the brother of a poet."

HERONGATE. Traditional English melody collected, arranged, and harmonized by Ralph Vaughan Williams. *See No. 17.*

241   In the Bleak Midwinter

Christina Georgina Rossetti (1830-1894) was an English poet, known for short, intense lyrics such as these. She was the daughter of the exiled Italian patriot and writer Gabriele Rossetti, and the sister of Dante Gabriel Rossetti, poet and painter. Her works include *Goblin Market and Other Poems*, 1862; *The Prince's Progress and Other Poems*, 1866; and books of devotional poetry and prose. Verse 1 is taken from Rossetti's "A Christmas Carol"; Verses 2 and 3 include new words by John Andrew Storey. *See No. 2.*

CRANHAM. Gustav Theodore Holst (1874-1934), English composer, arranged this melody, which appeared in Theodoric Petri's *Piae Cantiones*, 1582. *See No. 249.* A pupil of Sir Charles Stanford (*see No. 36*) at the Royal College of Music, where he later taught, Holst directed music for more than twenty-five years at St. Paul's School for Girls and Morley College, London. His compositions included instrumental and choral music, operas, and works inspired by the English folk song tradition.

242   In the Lonely Midnight

Theodore Chickering Williams (1855-1915) was an American Unitarian minister who served the Unitarian Church of All Souls, New York City, from 1883 to 1896. He published a metrical translation of Virgil's *Aeneid* and edited with his wife, Velma C. Williams, *Hymnal: Amore Dei*, 1890.

This hymn first appeared in *The New Hymn and Tune Book*, 1914. The original lines 2 and 8, stanza 3, are "Sent from heaven on high," and "Christ your king is born."

> ADORO TE DEVOTE. French melody. This tune was adapted for *Hymns for the Celebration of Life*, 1964, from the version of the plainsong melody used by the monks of Solesmes, France.

243   Jesus, Our Brother
French carol (12th century) based on Luke 2:7; the translation is anonymous.

> ORIENTIS PARTIBUS. Medieval French melody (12th century). This harmony is by Carlton R. Young. *See No. 18.*

244   It Came upon the Midnight Clear
Edmund Hamilton Sears (1810-1876), a Unitarian minister, served several congregations in Massachusetts. The author of many books, hymns, and poems, he is chiefly remembered for two Christmas hymns, "Calm on the listening ear of night" and this one. This hymn was reportedly written at the request of his friend, W. P. Lunt, minister in Quincy, Massachusetts, where it was introduced at the 1849 Sunday School Christmas celebration. Percy Dearmer, in his *Songs of Praise Discussed*, 1933, notes "that most Victorian hymnbooks offered little or no application of the social message of Christmas— 'Peace on earth, goodwill towards men.' The hymns that began to express the teachings of Christ came from New England, and it is notable that this one was written by a Unitarian minister."

> CAROL. Richard Storrs Willis (1819-1900) arranged this tune, which appeared in Study 23 of his *Church Chorals and Choir Studies*, 1850. Born in Boston, Willis was a pupil of Felix Mendelssohn (*see No. 11*) and others during six years in Europe, and a prominent music critic and publisher in New York.

245   Joy to the World
Isaac Watts (1674-1748), an English independent or Congregationalist minister, was a pioneer in emancipating English-speaking churches from a hymnody consisting almost exclusively of psalms in rhyme. His psalms and freely composed hymns became immensely popular in England and America. A liberal, Watts wrote, "I hate these shackles of the mind./ Forg'd by the haughty wise;/ Souls were not born to be confin'd,/ And led, like Samson, blind and bound." This text is in part a paraphrase of Psalm 98. Here it is altered in a few places, notably the use of "Word" instead of "Lord" in the first verse.

COMFORT. This tune first appeared in *Methodist Collection of Tunes,* 1833. This tune is not an arrangement in the usual sense, however, but a development of the four-note motive used for the opening syllables of the chorus, "Glory to God," in George Frederick Handel's *Messiah,* 1742.

246   O Little Town of Bethlehem
Phillips Brooks (1835-1893) was a great preacher of the American Episcopal church and one of the most influential ministers of his day. As rector of Philadelphia's Holy Trinity Church, he wrote this Christmas text for his Sunday school in 1868, after a visit to Israel. The next year Brooks became rector of Trinity Church, Boston, and in 1891, bishop of Massachusetts.

ST. LOUIS. Lewis H. Redner (1831-1908), a Philadelphian, was a real estate broker, Sunday school superintendent, and the organist at Phillips Brooks's Holy Trinity Church. He composed this tune to fit the text "O Little Town of Bethlehem."

247   O Little Town of Bethlehem
Phillips Brooks. *See No. 246.*

FOREST GREEN. *See No. 57.* English melody, harmonized by Ralph Vaughan Williams. *See No. 17.* This tune is an alternative to the one commonly used in the United States.

248   O We Believe in Christmas
Percival Chubb (1860-1960) was a founder of the Fellowship of the New Life, a precursor of the Fabian Society, one of the oldest socialist societies of Great Britain. Born in Devonshire, England, Chubb was reared in the Anglican church, but he was greatly influenced by Emerson and decided to join the American ethical movement. He helped organize the Ethical Society in London, then moved to New York to teach at the Ethical Culture School. He became well known for using drama in class to encourage students' interest in literature. He was the founder of the Drama League of America, which encouraged production of plays and increased the public demand for plays to be published.

ADLER. American folk hymn melody in *The Revivalist,* 1868.

249   On This Day Everywhere
Piae Cantiones, 1582, was a remarkable collection of medieval sacred and secular songs gathered and edited by Theodoric Petri, a Finnish student at the University of Rostock, Denmark, then part of the Swedish kingdom. In 1591 Petri became secretary to Sigismund, king of Sweden; little else is

known of him save that he spent his late years in Poland. The single extant copy of Petri's collection was taken to England about 1852 by the British minister to Sweden. This version of this hymn text was created by Vincent B. Silliman (*see No. 42*) and the Reverend Christopher Moore (1929-1987), a Unitarian Universalist who served congregations in St. Louis, Missouri, and Chicago and was the founding director of the Chicago Children's Choir. He was a member of the commission that compiled *Hymns for the Celebration of Life*, 1964.

PERSONENT HODIE. Gustav Theodore Holst. *See No. 241.*

250   purer than purest

e. e. cummings (1894-1962), a Unitarian poet and painter, was born in Cambridge, Massachusetts, the son of a Unitarian minister. During World War I, while driving for a French ambulance service, he was detained on suspicion of treason and held in a French internment camp. Between the ages of eighteen and twenty-four, cummings is said to have written one poem per day. Later, he published plays, prose, and twelve volumes of poetry; his *Complete Poems* were published posthumously in 1968. This text is taken, with minor alterations, from "purer than purest pure" in *XAIPE*, 1950.

STAR. Vincent Persichetti (1915-1988) was a composer and pianist who served on the faculties of the Philadelphia Conservatory and the Julliard School of Music. He composed several symphonies, string quartets, and piano sonatas. This tune is from his collection of hymn tunes, *Hymns and Responses for the Church Year*, 1956.

251   Silent Night, Holy Night

Joseph Mohr (1792-1848) was an Austrian Roman Catholic priest who, as assistant priest of the parish church at Oberndorf, collaborated with organist Franz Xavier Gruber on this hymn for Christmas Eve, 1818. The translator of this familiar version is unknown.

STILLE NACHT. Franz Xavier Gruber (1787-1863), a composer, was the son of a poor linen weaver, born in Upper Austria. He was organist at Saint Nikolaus Church in Oberndorf and, later, headmaster at Berndorf and organist at Hallein, near Salzburg.

252   Stille Nacht

Joseph Mohr. *See No. 251.*

STILLE NACHT. Franz Xavier Gruber. *See No. 251.*

253   O Come, All Ye Faithful
John Francis Wade (1711-1786), an English Roman Catholic, may have written this beloved Christmas carol between 1740 and 1743. Wade, a music copyist, was a politico-religious refugee in Douai, France, where he made hymn collections for Roman Catholic family chapels. The earliest extant copies of this text are in his script. This translation is based upon that of Frederick Oakeley (1802-1880) and others. Oakeley was an English Anglican who late in life converted to Roman Catholicism.

>   ADESTE FIDELES. John Francis Wade (1711-1786) composed or at least transcribed this tune, which was found in a manuscript written by him. It is a "fuguing tune" of the type common in England and the United States in the eighteenth century, with the soprano imitated by the tenor in the refrain.

254   Sing We Now of Christmas
Traditional French carol.

>   NOEL NOUVELET. Medieval French carol, harmonized by Marcel Dupré (1886-1971). Dupré, an organist and composer, was born in Rouen, France. Born into a family of musicians, Dupré was appointed organist of St. Vivien's Chapel at the age of twelve. He later became professor at the Paris conservatoire and chief organist at St. Sulpice Church, Paris, and Notre Dame Cathedral. In 1939 Dupré went on his first world tour and in 1953 celebrated his 1,900th concert.

255   There's a Star in the East
African American spiritual (ca. 1750-1875) that comes from traditional biblical text. A "map song" (*see No. 116*), it directs runaway slaves to follow the North Star to safety.

>   DOUGLASS. African American spiritual (ca. 1750-1875). This tune is named for Frederick Douglass. *See No. 579.*

256   Winter Night
Shelley Jackson Denham. *See No. 55.*

>   WINTER LULLABY. Shelley Jackson Denham. *See No. 55.*

257   'Twas in the Moon of Wintertime
Jean de Brébeuf (1593-1649), a French Jesuit priest, founded a mission among the Huron people of the Saint Lawrence River Valley in Canada, from whom this text is derived. The translation is by Jesse Edgar Middleton (1872-1960).

>   JESOUS AHATONHIA. Canadian carol, arranged by H. Barrie Cabena (1933-).

258 Whence, O Shepherd Maiden?

French Canadian carol (ca.1700).

D'OU VIENS TU, BERGERE. French Canadian carol (ca. 1700).

259 We Three Kings of Orient Are

John Henry Hopkins Jr. (1820-1891), a US Episcopal cleric, led in the development of hymnody in that denomination during the mid-nineteenth century. He created this Epiphany carol in 1857. In 1863 it appeared in his *Carols, Hymns and Songs*. The last stanza is by Vincent B. Silliman. *See No. 42.*

KINGS OF ORIENT. John Henry Hopkins Jr. (1820-1891).

260 Oshana, Shira Oshana

Echoing Psalm 118:26 and Mark 11:9, this text can be translated, "Hosanna! Blessed is the one who comes in the name of the Lord."

HEVENU. Traditional Hebrew.

261 When Jesus Wept

William Billings (1746-1800), a self-taught musician from Boston, Massachusetts, wrote "fuguing tunes" in which melodies are repeated by different voices. Known for writing choral music in support of the American Revolution, he published *The New England Psalm-Singer* in 1770 and *The Singing Master's Assistant* in 1778. Billings's appealing music and style of teaching enabled him to help others to sing and appreciate his tunes.

WHEN JESUS WEPT. William Billings (1746-1800).

262 Hosanna in the Highest

John Howland Lathrop (1880-1967) was minister of the First Unitarian Congregational Society in Brooklyn, New York, for more than forty years. In 1956, he received the American Unitarian Association's Award for Distinguished Service to the Cause of Unitarian Universalism. This hymn, here with one stanza removed, was used for a Palm Sunday procession.

ELLACOMBE. This tune is varied slightly from the setting of "Der du im heil'gsten Sakrament" in Xavier Ludwig Hartig's *Vollständige Sammlung der gewöhnlichen Melodien zum Mainzer Gesangbuche*, Mainz, Germany, around 1833. That, in turn, was much altered from an earlier melody in *Gesang-Buch...der herzogl Wirtembergischen katholischen Hofkapelle*, 1784.

263   When Jesus Looked from Olivet
Mark L. Belletini. *See No. 73.*

> WHEN JESUS WEPT. William Billings. *See No. 261.* This tune was harmonized by Richard D. Wetzel in 1972.

264   Now in the Tomb Is Laid
Padraic Colum (1881-1972), an Irish-born Roman Catholic poet, came to America in 1914. He received, among other honors, the Academy of American Poets Award in 1952. This text is No. 14 of a series written for the stations of the cross—created in bronze by sculptor Alfeo Faggi—in St. Thomas's Roman Catholic Church, Chicago. It was published in the booklet *The Way of the Cross*, 1926.

> COLUM. Gerald Kechley, a Unitarian Universalist, is professor emeritus of the School of Music, University of Washington, Seattle. He is director of music at the East Shore Unitarian Church, Bellevue, Washington.

265   O Sacred Head, Now Wounded
Bernard of Clairvaux (1091-1153) is believed to have written "Rhythmica Oratio," the Latin text on which this text is based. Its final section, "Salve caput cruentatum," was freely translated by German Lutheran hymn writer Paulus Gerhardt (1607-1676) to create this Good Friday text. This English version was created by James Waddell Alexander (1804-1859), a US cleric who taught at Princeton University and was minister of the Fifth Avenue Presbyterian Church in New York. This hymn was first published in *The Christian Lyre*, 1830.

> PASSION CHORALE. Hans Leo Hassler (*see No. 110*) composed this tune for the love song "Mein G'muth ist mir verwirret" in his *Lustgarten neurer teutscher Gesäng*, 1601. This melody, applied to Christoph Knoll's "Herzlich tut mich verlangen," 1613, and Paulus Gerhardt's "O Haupt voll Blut und Wunden," 1656, became known as the Passion Chorale. This version is one of five given in Johann Sebastian Bach's (*see No. 41*) *St. Matthew Passion*, 1729.

266   Now the Green Blade Riseth
John MacLeod Campbell Crum (1872-1958) was an Anglican priest. This springtime carol, written in the early twentieth century for Easter services, appears in altered form. The word "carol" originally meant "roundance," and songs so named were danced to as well as sung.

> NOEL NOUVELET. Medieval French carol, harmonized by Marcel Dupré. *See No. 254.*

267   When Mary through the Garden Went

Mary Coleridge (1861-1907) was a British educator and author. Widely known as a poet, Coleridge was also a successful novelist in the late 1800s. Her first novel, *The Seven Sleepers of Effuses*, and her first volume of poetry, *Fancy's Following*, 1896, were published under the name M. E. Coleridge. All of her subsequent works were published under the pseudonym Anodos. It was not until *Poems by Mary E. Coleridge* was published posthumously that the identity of Anodos was revealed.

WAS GOTT THUT. Severus Gastorius. *See No. 76.*

268   Jesus Christ Is Risen Today

Charles Wesley (1707-1788) was a British Methodist evangelist and hymn writer; his brother John was the founder of Methodism. It is estimated that Wesley wrote at least 6,500 hymns in his lifetime, including "Hark! The Herald Angels Sing" and "Love Divine, All Loves Excelling." This text has been altered.

EASTER HYMN. *See No. 61.*

269   Lo, the Day of Days Is Here

Frederick Lucian Hosmer. *See No. 45.* First published in *Hymns for the Celebration of Life*, 1964, this text combines portions of two of Hosmer's hymns to provide a new Easter text stressing the rebirth of nature.

LLANFAIR. Robert Williams (ca. 1781-1821) was a blind basketmaker in Anglesey, an island northwest of Wales. This melody was included in a manuscript dated 1817. The harmony, from John Parry's *Peroriaeth Hyfryd*, 1837, is by John Roberts (Henllan).

270   O Day of Light and Gladness

Frederick Lucian Hosmer. *See No. 45.* This Easter hymn, written in 1903, was published in Louisa Loring's *Hymns of the Ages*, 1904, and slightly revised in *Unity Hymns and Chorals*, 1911.

LANCASHIRE. Henry Smart (1813-1879), organist at Blackburn, Lancashire, England, composed this tune for the text "From Greenland's icy mountains," for a missionary meeting in 1836. That year he returned to his native London, where he was long active as organist and organ designer. The tune was introduced in *Psalms and Hymns for Divine Worship*, 1867.

271 Come Down, O Love Divine
Bianco da Siena (d. 1434?) was a monk. This text was translated by Richard
Frederick Littledale (1833-1890) and has been altered for this collection.
> DOWN AMPNEY. Ralph Vaughan Williams. *See No. 17.*

272 O Prophet Souls of All the Years
Frederick Lucian Hosmer. *See No. 45.* This hymn was written for the 1893
World Parliament of Religions in Chicago and was included in *The Thought
of God, Second Series,* 1894, as "One Law, One Life, One Love." Lines 2
and 4 of the first stanza ("Bend o'er us from above," and "Now to fulfill-
ment move,") and line 4 of the third stanza ("The Spirit's tongue of flame")
have been changed.
> BANGOR. From W. Tans'ur's *Compleat Melody,* 1735. This tune was
> harmonized by John Wilson (1905-1992), a composer best known
> in North America for his hymn tune "Lauds." From 1965 to 1980
> he taught at the Royal College of Music.

273 Immortal, Invisible
Walter Chalmers Smith (1824-1908) was minister of the Free High Church
of Edinburgh and moderator of the Assembly of the Free Church of Scotland. This text, based on I Timothy 1:17, first appeared in Smith's *Hymns
of Christ and the Christian Life,* 1867. Here, the third and fourth stanzas
of the original have been combined.
> ST. DENIO. *See No. 122.*

274 Dear Mother-Father of Us All
John Greenleaf Whittier. *See No. 9.* This text is based on the concluding
stanzas of "The Brewing of Soma," which describe the East Indian practice
of drinking intoxicating soma to commune with deity. Many Christians,
Whittier says, symbolically brew "the heathen soma still." Here, the poet
sets forth what he sees as a better and more natural way to converse with
God. This text has been altered.
> REST. Frederick Charles Maker (1844-1927) was a Congregational
> organist who lived in Bristol, England. This tune, written in 1887,
> was composed for Whittier's text and appeared in G. S. Barnett's
> *Congregational Hymnal.*

275 Joyful Is the Dark
Brian Wren. *See No. 23.*
> LINDNER. Carlton R. Young. *See No. 18.*

276   O Young and Fearless Prophet
Samuel Ralph Harlow (1885-1972) was a Congregational minister and educator from Massachusetts. He served as chaplain and head of the Sociology Department at the International College, Smyrna, Turkey; as general secretary of the Student Volunteer Movement for the Near East; and as the New England field secretary of the American Board of Commissioners for Foreign Missions. In 1923 he joined the Smith College Department of Religion. This text has been altered.

> MEIRIONYDD. William Lloyd. *See No. 40.*

277   When We Wend Homeward
Adapted from Psalm 126.

> LAND OF REST. US folk melody, arranged by Annabel Morris Buchanan. *See No. 70.*

278   Praise Be to God, the Almighty
Joachim Neander (1650-1680) was a German pietistic preacher, scholar, teacher, poet, and musician. Discharged as headmaster of the Reformed Grammar School at Düsseldorf, he lived for some time in a cave on the Rhine still known as Neander's Cave. In Neanderthal, the valley of that cave, were found the skeletal remains of Neanderthal Man in 1856. Neander was for a brief time a controversial second preacher at St. Martin's in Bremen. He wrote sixty hymns with tunes that were published the year he died. This version, based on the translation of Catherine Winkworth (*see No. 32*) of Neander's text beginning, "Lobe den Herren, den mächtigen König der Ehren!" comes from *Hymns of the Spirit*, 1937, and is based on Psalm 103:1-6 and Psalm 150.

> LOBE DEN HERREN. Originally used for "Hast du denn, Liebster" in the *Ander Theil des Erneuerten Gesangbuchs*, Stralsund, 1665, this tune has been associated with Neander's text since 1680. This version accompanies Catherine Winkworth's translation in her *Chorale Book for England*, 1863.

279   By the Waters of Babylon
Psalm 137:1. The words to this round express the longing of the exiled Jewish people for their homeland.

> UNKNOWN. This tune is frequently attributed, erroneously, to William Billings. *See No. 261.*

280 Haleluhu

Traditional Hebrew, from Psalm 150:5-6. The text can be translated, "Praise God with loud, high-sounding cymbals. Let all who have breath praise the Lord. Hallelujah."

> HALELUHU. Traditional Hebrew melody arranged by Mark Slegers (1948-), music director of the First Unitarian Church, Portland, Oregon. Slegers was a member of the Hymnbook Resources Commission, which compiled *Singing the Living Tradition.*

281 O God, Our Help in Ages Past

Isaac Watts. *See No. 245.* Many would call this paraphrase of Psalm 90 the greatest hymn in English.

> ST. ANNE. William Croft (1676-1727), English organist and composer, first published this tune anonymously in the sixth edition of the *Supplement to the New Version of Psalms,* 1708. The leading Anglican musician of his generation, Croft succeeded his master, Dr. John Blow (1649-1708), as organist of Westminster Abbey and choirmaster of the Chapel Royal. The hardy first phrase of this tune is a stock melody also used by English composer Henry Lawes and by George Frederick Handel. The Bach fugue beginning with that phrase is known in England as the "St. Anne's Fugue."

282 Let the Whole Creation Cry

Stopford Augustus Brooke (1832-1916), a prominent preacher, was born at Letterkenny, Donegal, Ireland, and ordained in London. In 1872 he was appointed chaplain to Queen Victoria; she offered him the canonry of Westminster, but his liberal views made accepting the position impossible. In 1880 he resigned from the Anglican ministry and officiated at Bedford Chapel, Bloomsbury, as a Unitarian until 1894. This hymn is loosely based on Psalm 148 and has been arranged and adapted from a longer text.

> ST. GEORGE'S WINDSOR. George Job Elvey. *See No. 68.*

283 The Spacious Firmament on High

Joseph Addison (1672-1719) was a British essayist, politician, and poet. He was a major contributor to *The Spectator,* 1711-1712, for which he provided 274 of the 555 daily issues. He held a number of diplomatic positions, including secretary of state, and wrote operas and plays. This text, a paraphrase of Psalm 19:1-6, first appeared in *The Spectator.* It has been included in Episcopal hymnals since 1789, and American Unitarians and Universalists have been singing it for generations.

CREATION. Franz Joseph Haydn. *See No. 81.* Adapted from the chorus of "The heavens are telling" in Haydn's *The Creation*, 1798, this tune can be found in *Dulcimer, or New York Collection of Sacred Music*, 1850.

284   Praise, O My Heart, to You

Ridgely Torrence (1875-1950), a US poet and playwright, was an editor of *The New Republic* from 1920 to 1934. This hymn was drawn from "Adam's Song of the Visible World," a poem reminiscent of Psalm 104.

ADAM'S SONG. Robert L. Sanders. *See No. 5.*

285   We Worship Thee, God

Sir Robert Grant (1779-1838), composer and public servant, was born in India. He served in Parliament and was appointed governor of Bombay in 1834. Many of his hymns were published in India the year after his death. This hymn, based on Psalm 104, is widely used. Here it has been recast.

LYONS. From Volume II of *Sacred Melodies from Haydn, Mozart, and Beethoven*, 1815, edited by William Gardiner (1770-1853). Gardiner is credited with introducing the music of Ludwig van Beethoven (*see No. 29*) to England. A successful hosiery manufacturer, he told of sending stockings to Franz Joseph Haydn with the recipient's melodies, including "Austria," woven into the design. Gardiner credits Haydn (*see No. 81*) with the subject of this tune, which was a widely used musical phrase. A number of minuets by Joseph or Michael Haydn begin with it, as does "Hanover" by William Croft (*see No. 281*), 1708.

286   A Core of Silence

Jim Reilly (1943-) is a musician. This hymn was written for use at the First Universalist Church of Minneapolis, where he was director of music from 1979 to 1988. It appears in *Songs for Anything*, 1986.

TRUE RELIGION. Jim Reilly (1943-).

287   Faith of the Larger Liberty

Vincent B. Silliman. *See No. 42.* This hymn was written for a 1944 institute of Middle Atlantic States Unitarian ministers. It was published in *We Sing of Life*, 1955.

MIT FREUDEN ZART. A Bohemian Brethren tune published in *Kirchengeseng darinnen die Heubtartickel des christlichen Glaubens gefasset*, 1566, reminiscent of the tune used for Psalm

138 in the Genevan Psalter of 1543 and of "Une pastourelle gentille," a song published by Attaignant (1529-1530).

288 All Are Architects

Henry Wadsworth Longfellow. *See No. 240.* This hymn consists of stanzas 1, 3, and 8 of "The Builders."

WOODLAND. Thomas Benjamin. *See No. 2.*

289 Creative Love, Our Thanks We Give

William DeWitt Hyde (1858-1917), Congregational minister and author, became president of Bowdoin College in 1855 and served there for thirty-two years. Hyde's text was adapted by Beth Ide (1921-), a Unitarian Universalist minister of religious education who has served congregations in Athens and Mason, Georgia; Providence, Rhode Island; and Boulder, Colorado.

TRUTH FROM ABOVE. English melody, harmonized by Ralph Vaughan Williams. *See No. 17.*

290 Bring, O Past, Your Honor

Charles H. Lyttle (1884-1980) was a Unitarian minister who served congregations in Massachusetts, New York, Nebraska, and Illinois. In 1925, he joined the faculty of Meadville Theological School and taught church history there for many years. Lyttle was the author of *The Liberal Gospel*, 1925, and *Freedom Moves West*, 1952. This text was written for the centennial of the Unitarian Society, Geneva, Illinois, and contains historical allusions to "Liberty, Holiness, and Love," the 1825 American Unitarian Association "motto," which was incorporated in the Geneva church's constitution in 1842 and inscribed over its pulpit. The church bell is inscribed, "Praise to the Highest, peace to men below." The building's fieldstone walls—twenty inches thick—are, indeed, "stalwart."

NICAEA. John Bacchus Dykes. *See No. 26.*

291 Die Gedanken Sind Frei

German folk song. The English translation is by Arthur Kevess (verse 1) and Elizabeth Bennett (verses 2 and 3).

DIE GEDANKEN SIND FREI. Alsatian folk tune.

292 If I Can Stop One Heart from Breaking

Emily Dickinson (1830-1886) was a US poet who composed more than 1,000 works in her lifetime. Beginning in her twenties, she chose a life of seclusion, rarely leaving her Amherst, Massachusetts, home. Her epigrammatic, deceptively simple poems were published in several volumes after her death and have had considerable influence on modern poetry. This poem was written ca. 1864 and published in 1890.

SMIT. Leo Smit (1921-) is a Philadelphia-born pianist and composer. After his debut on piano at Carnegie Hall in 1939, he became a teacher of music at several institutions and later toured Latin America, giving concerts of North American music. His compositions are mainly neoclassical in style. This tune was commissioned for *Singing the Living Tradition*.

293 O Star of Truth

Minot Judson Savage. *See No. 77*. This text was abridged and revised for *Hymns for the Celebration of Life*, 1964.

NYLAND. Finnish folk melody from the village of Kuortane. This tune became a Lutheran hymn tune in the appendix to the *Suomen Evankelis Luterilaisen Kirken Koraalikirja*, 1909. This tune was adapted by David Evans (*see No. 38*) and appears here in simplified form.

294 Our Praise We Give

John Coleman Adams (1849-1922) was a Universalist minister who held pastorates in Massachusetts, Illinois, New York, and Connecticut. Author of several hymns, he wrote this text for a church anniversary. It appeared in *The New Hymn and Tune Book*, 1914, with five stanzas; these are the first three, slightly altered.

GONFALON ROYAL. Percy Carter Buck. *See No. 58*.

295 Sing Out Praises for the Journey

Mark M. DeWolfe (1953-1988) was a Unitarian Universalist minister at the Unitarian Congregation of South Peel, Mississauga, Ontario. This text was revised by Joyce Painter Rice, a Unitarian Universalist and former music director for the Arlington Street Church, Boston.

WESTMINSTER ABBEY. Henry Purcell (1659-1695) has been described as the greatest English composer of his period. He wrote the first important English opera, *Dido and Aeneas*, in 1689, as well as church and other music. He served as organist in Westminster Abbey and in 1682 became organist at the Chapel Royal.

296 O Ye Who Taste That Love Is Sweet

Christina Georgina Rossetti. *See No. 241*. This hymn is the last three stanzas of "What Good Shall My Life Do to Me."

O FILII ET FILIAE. French melody (ca. 1500). This tune is probably the original melody for the text written by Jean Tisserand, a Franciscan monk, who died in Paris in 1494. The melody was first printed in *Airs sur les hymnes sacrez, odes et noèls*, Paris, 1623. It was harmonized thus for *Hymns for the Celebration of Life*, 1964.

297   The Star of Truth
John Andrew Storey. *See No. 2.*
> MCNAUGHTON. Dede Duson. *See No. 133.* This tune was commissioned for *Singing the Living Tradition.*

298   Wake, Now, My Senses
Thomas J. S. Mikelson (1936-), born in Iowa, is a Unitarian Universalist minister. He has served congregations in Iowa City, Iowa, and Brookline and Dedham, Massachusetts, and is serving the First Parish Church in Cambridge, Massachusetts. This hymn was written for the ordination and installation of Charity Rowley as minister of religious education in the First Parish Church of Arlington, Massachusetts.
> SLANE. Traditional Irish melody, harmonized by Carlton R. Young. *See No. 18.*

299   Make Channels for Streams of Love
Richard Chenevix Trench (1807-1886), Dublin-born author and cleric, became professor of divinity in King's College, dean of Westminster, and archbishop of Dublin. He wrote prolifically on history, literature, philology, the Bible, and theology. The poem from which this text, based on II Kings 4:1-7, is taken begins, "Pour forth the oil—pour boldly forth;/ It will not fail, until/ Thou failest vessels to provide/ Which it may largely fill." Line 2 of stanza 3 originally read, "That blessing from above."
> LAND OF REST. US folk melody. This arrangement is by Annabel Morris Buchanan with harmonization by Charles Webb. *See No. 70.*

300   With Heart and Mind
Alicia S. Carpenter. *See No. 6.* This text was commissioned for the Service of the Living Tradition.
> MACH'S MIT MIR GOTT. Johann Hermann Schein. *See No. 183.* The harmony is by J. S. Bach. *See No. 41.*

301   Touch the Earth, Reach the Sky!
Grace Lewis-McLaren. *See No. 73.* This text was written to celebrate the theme of the 1988 General Assembly in Palm Springs, California, where it was sung at the opening ceremony.

TOUCH THE EARTH. Grace Lewis-McLaren. *See No. 73.*

302   Children of the Human Race
John Andrew Storey. *See No. 2.*

LEE. Thomas Oboe Lee. *See No. 13.*

303   We Are the Earth Upright and Proud
Kenneth L. Patton (1911-1994) was a Unitarian Universalist minister who served congregations in Illinois, Wisconsin, Massachusetts, and New Jersey. One of the compilers of *Hymns for the Celebration of Life*, 1964, Patton wrote thirteen of the hymns and twenty-seven of the readings in that hymnal. He also published six volumes of poetry including *Beyond Doubt*, 1946, and *Man's Hidden Search*, 1954, and was editor of *Readings for the Celebration of Life*, 1957. In 1986, he won the Award for Distinguished Service to the Cause of Unitarian Universalism. This text, already widely used, was first published in *We Sing of Life*, 1955, in which the opening line reads, "Man is the earth upright and proud."

EIN' FESTE BURG. Martin Luther. *See No. 200.* The harmony is by J. S. Bach. *See No. 41.*

304   A Fierce Unrest
Don Marquis (1878-1937) was a US journalist and humorist, best known for his satirical poem *Archy and Mehitabel*. He also wrote serious poetry and drama and left an incomplete autobiography, *Sons of the Puritans*, 1939. This poem, found in many anthologies, may be the most quoted of his serious verse.

SALVATION. From Ananias Davisson's *Kentucky Harmony*, ca. 1815.

305   De Colores
David Arkin. *See No. 173.*

DE COLORES. Traditional Spanish folk tune, arranged by Betty A. Wylder. *See No. 109.*

306   Sing of Living, Sing of Dying
Thomas J. S. Mikelson. *See No. 298.*

ENOCH. Weldon Frederick Wooden. *See No. 3.* This tune was named in memory of his son, Enoch Wooden.

307   The Human Touch Can Light the Flame
John Andrew Storey. *See No. 2.*
>DICKINSON COLLEGE. Lee Hastings Bristol Jr. (1923-1979).

308   The Blessings of the Earth and Sky
Kenneth L. Patton. *See No. 303.* This text was written in 1951 for the dedication of the meetinghouse designed by Frank Lloyd Wright for the First Unitarian Society of Madison, Wisconsin. It was published in *Man Is the Meaning*, 1956.
>MACH'S MIT MIR GOTT. Johann Hermann Schein. *See No. 183.*

309   Earth Is Our Homeland
Mark L. Belletini (*see No. 73*) and Helen R. Pickett (1929-), who was born in Durban, Natal, South Africa, the daughter of Congregational missionaries to the Zulus. A lifelong church musician, she is married to O. Eugene Pickett, fourth president of the Unitarian Universalist Association. She is the editor of *Rejoice Together*, 1995, and was a member of the Hymnbook Resources Commission, which compiled *Singing the Living Tradition.*
>SYMPHONY. Johannes Brahms (1833-1897) was a leading composer of romantic symphonies, concertos, and chamber music. He ranks among the greatest of all creators of *lieder* (German art songs). Many feel that his greatest contribution to music is his original handling of variation techniques, in which he repeats a musical idea with slight changes. This tune was arranged by Fred Bock (1939-).

310   The Earth Is Home
Kenneth L. Patton. *See No. 303.* This hymn was first published in Patton's *Man Is the Meaning*, 1956, as one of a group of "Anthems of Humanity." The stanzas have been slightly rearranged.
>ALBRIGHT. William Albright. *See No. 43.* This tune was commissioned by Trinity Church, New York, for the Association of Anglican Musicians in 1973.

311   Let It Be a Dance
Ric Masten (1929-), a Unitarian Universalist, was ordained as a minister-at-large in 1971. From 1971 to 1983 he served as the Unitarian Universalist Association's Billings Lecturer, sharing his poems and music with thousands of Unitarian Universalists.
>MASTEN. Ric Masten's (1929-) tune was arranged by Betty A. Wylder. *See No. 109.*

312   Here on the Paths of Every Day
Edwin Markham. *See No. 177.* This text is an arrangement of twelve lines of "Earth Is Enough," first published in *The Shoes of Happiness and Other Poems*, 1916.

FILLMORE. From William Walker's *The Southern Harmony. See No. 15.*

313   O What a Piece of Work Are We
Malvina Reynolds (1900-1978), a Unitarian Universalist, was a radical political lyricist. Blacklisted for her outspoken political views, she was unable to find a teaching position, and so she earned a living as a tailor, social worker, and steelworker. She wrote more than 500 songs about women, children, technology, the environment, and peace, continuing to perform into her mid-seventies. Harry Belafonte, Joan Baez, and Pete Seeger are among the artists who have recorded her music.

DOVE OF PEACE. From William Walker's *The Southern Harmony. See No. 15.* Harmonized by Charles H. Webb. *See No. 70.*

314   We Are Children of the Earth
Alicia S. Carpenter. *See No. 6.* This text was commissioned for *Singing the Living Tradition.*

CON X'OM LANG. Nguyen-Duc Quang. *See No. 59.*

315   This Old World
US folk song, adapted.

RESTORATION. From William Walker's *The Southern Harmony. See No. 15.*

316   Tradition Held Fast
Jim Scott. *See No. 167.*

CIRCLE OF SPIRIT. Jim Scott. *See No. 167.*

317   We Are Not Our Own
Brian Wren. *See No. 23.*

NEXUS. David Hurd. *See No. 50.*

318   We Would Be One
Samuel Anthony Wright (1919-) is a biologist and minister emeritus of the Marin Fellowship of Unitarians in San Rafael, California. He has served congregations in California, Alaska, Texas, and Oklahoma. He has worked as director of American Unitarian Youth; director of Liberal Religious Youth,

Inc.; and director for the Department of In-Service Education at Starr King School for the Ministry. This text was written to accompany the tune "Sibelius" for Unitarian and Universalist youth at their Continental Convention of 1953-1954. At this conference they merged to form the Liberal Religious Youth of the United States and Canada, setting a model for the Unitarian Universalist denominational consolidation in 1961.

FINLANDIA. Jean Sibelius. *See No. 159.*

319 Ye Earthborn Children of a Star

John Godfrey MacKinnon (1903-1983) served Unitarian and Unitarian Universalist congregations in Illinois, Kansas, Virginia, Delaware, Pennsylvania, and Indiana.

GREENVILLE. Dede Duson. *See No. 133.* This tune was commissioned for *Singing the Living Tradition.*

320 The Pen Is Greater

John Andrew Storey. *See No. 2.*

GRAGARETH. David Dawson. *See No. 8.*

321 Here in the Flesh Is All That We Can Know

John Masefield (1878-1967) was an English poet, playwright, and novelist. A sailor in his youth, he is perhaps best known for his poems about the sea. He was England's poet laureate from 1930 until his death. This text is adapted from a sonnet beginning "Here in the self is all that man can know," published in Masefield's *Poems*, 1953.

SONG SPRINGS. T. J. Anderson (1928-), composer, attends the Eno River Unitarian Universalist Fellowship in Durham, North Carolina. Before his retirement, he was chair of the Music Department at Tufts University in Medford, Massachusetts. He began his career as a jazz musician and bandleader, performing with such stars as Charlie Mingus and Daniel Richmond. His orchestration of the Scott Joplin opera "Treemonisha" premiered in Atlanta, Georgia, in 1972. He was a member of the Hymnbook Resources Commission, which compiled *Singing the Living Tradition.*

322 Thanks Be for These

Richard Seward Gilbert (1936-) is the longtime minister of the First Unitarian Church in Rochester, New York. He won the Clarence R. Skinner Award in 1972 and 1973, and received the Angus H. MacLean Award in 1984 in acknowledgment of his work in religious education. He is the author of *In the Holy Quiet of This Hour*, 1995. Joyce Timmerman Gilbert

(1936-) is a teacher and indexer, a fourth-generation Universalist, and founder of the Unitarian Universalist Musicians Network.

TRANSYLVANIA. Hungarian chorale tune (ca. 1600). This tune was provided with new words by Marton Palfi in his *Unitarius Egyhahazi Ekeneskönyv*, Cluj-Koloszvar, 1924. It was popular among Unitarians in Transylvania and Hungary. This arrangement by Robert L. Sanders (*see No. 5*) appeared, in a different key, in *Hymns of the Spirit*, 1937.

323   Break Not the Circle

Fred Kaan. *See No. 59.*

YADDO. Thomas Benjamin. *See No. 2.*

324   Where My Free Spirit Onward Leads

Alicia S. Carpenter. *See No. 6.* This text was commissioned for *Singing the Living Tradition.*

KINGSFOLD. Traditional English melody harmonized and arranged by Ralph Vaughan Williams. *See No. 17.*

325   Love Makes a Bridge

Brian Wren. *See No. 23.*

EMERY. Gerald Wheeler (b. 1929).

326   Let All the Beauty We Have Known

Dana McLean Greeley (1908-1986), a Unitarian Universalist minister, served congregations in Massachusetts and New Hampshire. He was president of the American Unitarian Association from 1958 to 1961, and president of the newly formed Unitarian Universalist Association from 1961 to 1969. In 1969 he received the Unitarian Universalist Association's Award for Distinguished Service, and in 1970 became president of the International Association for Religious Freedom.

DANBY. English melody adapted and harmonized by Ralph Vaughan Williams. *See No. 17.*

327   Joy, Thou Goddess

Friedrich Johann Christoph von Schiller (1759-1805) was a German dramatist, poet, and historian. Schiller studied law and medicine and served as a military surgeon in Stuttgart, but he fled after his incendiary play *Die Räuber* ("The Robbers") reached the stage, and he was forbidden to write more plays. His later works, including plays, poems, and books of history, illuminated themes of moral and political freedom. Although Schiller had no skill or appreciation for music, many composers, including Ludwig van Beethoven, Johannes Brahms, Felix Mendelssohn, Franz Schubert, Robert Schumann, and Piotr Tchaikovsky, drew upon his texts.

HYMN TO JOY. Ludwig van Beethoven. *See No. 29.*

328   I Sought the Wood in Summer
Willa Cather (1873-1947) was an American writer noted for her portrayals of immigrant life on the American frontier. Her novels included *O Pioneers!*, 1913; *My Ántonia*, 1918; and *One of Ours*, 1922, which won the Pulitzer Prize for Fiction. This text is an excerpt from "I Sought the World in Winter," published in *April Twilights*, 1903.

MERLE'S TUNE. Hal H. Hopson. *See No. 34.*

329   Life Has Loveliness To Sell
Sara Teasdale (1884-1933) was one of the most popular American poets of the early twentieth century. Born in St. Louis, Missouri, Teasdale was an intensely emotional writer whose work concentrated on themes of love, beauty, and death. Her books include *Rivers to the Sea*, 1915, and *Dark of the Moon*, 1926. She committed suicide in New York in 1933. This text was published as "Barter" in *Love Songs*, winner of the 1918 Pulitzer Prize for Poetry.

BLISS. Leo W. Collins (1925-) is director of music at the First and Second Church in Boston.

330   The Arching Sky of Morning Glows
Mark L. Belletini. *See No. 73.*

TALLIS' CANON. Thomas Tallis. *See No. 88.*

331   Life Is the Greatest Gift of All
William E. Oliver. This text was adapted by Waldemar Hille. *See No. 9.*

BROTHER JAMES' AIR. James Leith McBeth Bain (ca. 1840-1925). This tune was arranged by David Dawson. *See No. 8.*

332   Perfect Singer
George Kimmich Beach (1935-), a Unitarian Universalist minister, has served congregations in Austin, Texas; Cleveland, Ohio; Marblehead, Massachusetts; and Arlington, Virginia. He is the author of *If Yes Is the Answer, What Is the Question?*, 1995. These lines were written to accompany the chorale tune of Béla Bartók's *Concerto for Orchestra*, 1943.

CHORALE. Béla Bartók (1881-1945), Hungarian composer and pianist, was born in Transylvania and began composing at the age of nine.

He became interested in preserving folk music and traveled widely through Hungary and Romania, writing down and recording folk tunes. This music, along with the strong national movement in Hungary, greatly influenced his compositions, which include many works for piano, violin, and orchestra. During these years Bartók, a Unitarian, served as organist of the Unitarian Church in Budapest. In 1940 he emigrated to New York City, where his last years were spent in severe financial hardship because his royalties were cut off by World War II.

333   Alone She Cuts and Binds the Grain
William Wordsworth (1770-1850), with fellow poet Samuel Taylor Coleridge, launched the English Romantic movement. Born in the Lake District of northern England, he is best remembered for the lyrical and dramatic poems he published in *Lyrical Ballads*, 1798 and 1800, and *Poems, in Two Volumes*, 1807. Wordsworth became England's poet laureate in 1843.

DEVOTION. Allen D. Carden's *Missouri Harmony*, 1820.

334   When Shall We Learn
W(ystan) H(ugh) Auden (1907-1973) was a poet and literary figure. Born in York, England, he emigrated to the United States in 1939 and received US citizenship seven years later. In 1948 he won a Pulitzer Prize in poetry for *The Age of Anxiety*. Auden's oeuvre includes plays, opera librettos (including *The Rake's Progress*, 1951), essays, and numerous collections of poetry. This text is arranged from "Canzone," first published in *The Collected Poetry of W. H. Auden*, 1945.

FLENTGE. Carl Flentge Schalk (1929-) is a professor at Concordia University, River Forest, Illinois.

335   Once When My Heart Was Passion Free
John Banister Tabb (Father Tabb) (1845-1909) was a teacher, poet, and Roman Catholic priest born in Amelia County, Virginia. His poems, published in several collections, include "The Light of Bethlehem," "Out of Bounds," "The Sisters," and "Evolution."

PRIMROSE. From *Kentucky Harmony. See No. 186.*

336   All My Memories of Love
Anna Akhmatova (Anna Andreevna Gorenko) (1888-1966) was one of the greatest Russian poets of the twentieth century. Her poems, which explore religion, love, art, and other themes, include "Rekviem" ("Requiem") and

"Poema baz geroya" ("Poem without a Hero"). Ostracized and persecuted by Soviet authorities beginning in the 1920s, she was slowly rehabilitated after 1958. This text was translated by Mark L. Belletini. *See No. 73.*

ADORO TE DEVOTE. *See No. 242.*

337   Have I Not Known
Don Marquis. *See No. 304.*

> JERUSALEM. Charles Hubert Hastings Parry (1848-1918) was an English composer, scholar, and teacher whose ethical and aesthetic standards had great influence. He began publishing songs and church music in the 1870s and also composed oratorios, symphonies, and other works. In 1883 he joined the staff of the Royal College of Music, of which he eventually became director. Much of his work was collected into twelve volumes of English lyrics. This tune was arranged by Janet Wyatt (1934-).

338   I Seek the Spirit of a Child
Carl G. Seaburg. *See No. 37.* This text was commissioned for *Singing the Living Tradition.*

> SUSSEX CAROL. Traditional English melody, arranged and harmonized by Ralph Vaughan Williams. *See No. 17.*

339   Knowledge, They Say
Alfred Noyes (1880-1958) was an English poet who taught at Princeton University from 1914 to 1923. Reared a Protestant and influenced by Thomas H. Huxley's agnosticism, Noyes became a Roman Catholic in 1925. This text, arranged from Noyes's *Watchers of the Sky* by Kenneth L. Patton (*see No. 303*), was first published in *Hymns for the Celebration of Life,* 1964.

> SHELDONIAN. Cyril V. Taylor. *See No. 64.*

340   Though Gathered Here to Celebrate
Christine Doreian Michaels (1942-) is a psychologist and poet who attends the First Unitarian Church in Pittsburgh, Pennsylvania. This hymn was written after the death of a friend's husband.

> DISTANT BELOVED. Weldon Frederick Wooden. *See No. 3.*

341   O World, Thou Choosest Not the Better Part
George Santayana (1863-1952) was a poet and philosopher born in Madrid, Spain. His family came to the United States in 1872. Primarily known for his theories of aesthetics, morality, and the spiritual life, he taught phi-

losophy at Harvard for more than twenty years. His published works include *A Hermit of Carmel and Other Poems*, 1901, *The Life of Reason*, 1905-1906, and a novel, *The Last Puritan*, 1935.

SONG I. Orlando Gibbons (1583-1625), British composer of sacred and secular music, came from a respected family of musicians. He served as the organist of the Chapel Royal, chamber musician to the king, and organist at Westminster Abbey. This tune was harmonized by Ralph Vaughan Williams. *See No. 17.*

342   O Slowly, Slowly, They Return

Wendell Berry (1934-) is a US writer and farmer whose works illuminate the beauty and power of nature and promote the care of the earth. Born in Henry County, Kentucky, he taught at the University of Kentucky from 1964 to 1977. His numerous books of poetry, fiction, and nonfiction include *The Broken Ground*, 1964; *The Country of Marriage*, 1973; and *What Are People For?*, 1990. This text comes from *Sabbaths*, 1987.

SOLOTHURN. Swiss tune (1826).

343   A Firemist and a Planet

William Herbert Carruth (1859-1924) was an American educator and author.

NEW ENGLAND. New England folk melody.

344   A Promise through the Ages Rings

Alicia S. Carpenter. *See No. 6.*

WAS GOTT THUT. Severus Gastorius. *See No. 76.*

345   With Joy We Claim the Growing Light

Samuel Longfellow. *See No. 12.* This text is adapted from stanzas 3 and 4 of a five-stanza hymn beginning, "Eternal One, thou living God." It was written in 1875, possibly for the twenty-fifth anniversary of Preble Chapel in Portland, Maine.

WINCHESTER NEW. *See No. 145.*

346   Come, Sing a Song with Me

Carolyn McDade. *See No. 121.*

A ROSE IN WINTER. Carolyn McDade. *See No. 121.*

347   Gather the Spirit

Jim Scott. *See No. 167.*

GATHER THE SPIRIT. Jim Scott. *See No. 167.*

348   Guide My Feet
Traditional.

GUIDE MY FEET. Spiritual from the collection of Willis Laurence James (1900-1966). This tune was harmonized by Wendell Whalum. *See No. 141.*

349   We Gather Together
Dorothy Caiger Senghas (1930-), a librarian, attends the First Unitarian Universalist Society in Burlington, Vermont. Robert E. Senghas (1928-) is a Unitarian Universalist minister who served as the Unitarian Universalist Association's executive vice president from 1974 to 1979, and has served congregations in Wellesley Hills, Massachusetts; Davis, California; and Burlington, Vermont. This text was written for a Thanksgiving Sunday service.

KREMSER. *See No. 67.*

350   The Ceaseless Flow of Endless Time
John Andrew Storey. *See No. 2.*

MCKEE. African American spiritual (ca. 1750-1875), adapted and harmonized by Harry T. Burleigh. *See No. 148.*

351   A Long, Long Way the Sea-Winds Blow
William Stanley Braithwaite (1878-1962) was a poet, critic, and anthologist. A native of Boston, he served on the literary editorial staff of the *Boston Transcript* and later was on the faculty of the English Department at Atlanta University. In 1918 he was awarded the Spingarn Medal. As an African American poet, he is unusual in that none of his poetry was motivated by or refers to race.

LIVERPOOL. M. C. H. Davis, from *Southern Harmony*, 1835.

352   Find a Stillness
Carl G. Seaburg. *See No. 37.* This text is based on the words used with this tune in Transylvanian Unitarian churches.

SIGISMUND. Transylvanian hymn tune harmonized by Larry Phillips. *See No. 37.* This tune is named for John Sigismund, king of Transylvania (*see No. 37*).

353   Golden Breaks the Dawn
Chinese. Verse 1 comes from the Chinese of T. C. Chao (b. 1888), translated by Frank W. Price and Daniel Niles. Verse 2 is by John Andrew Storey. *See No. 2.*

LE PING. Hu Te-Ai (ca. 1900-). This tune was harmonized by David Dawson. *See No. 8.*

354   We Laugh, We Cry
Shelley Jackson Denham. *See No. 55.*
> CREDO. Shelley Jackson Denham's tune is harmonized by Betsy Jo Angebranndt. *See No. 28.*

355   We Lift Our Hearts in Thanks
Percival Chubb. *See No. 248.*
> PRAETORIOUS. From *Harmoniae Hymnorum Scholae Gorlicensis*, 1599.

356   Will You Seek in Far-Off Places?
Alicia S. Carpenter. *See No. 6.* These words were suggested by the Walt Whitman poem "Here and Now."
> GUTER HIRTE. This tune was added to the second edition of the *Geistreiches Gesangbuch*, 1705, compiled by Johann August Freylinghausen (1670-1739), who was a poet of the Pietist movement and preacher at Halle, Germany. That songbook was expanded to 1,588 hymns and 327 tunes and was widely used by immigrants to the United States. This arrangement is by Norman Luboff (1917-1987).

357   Bright Morning Stars Are Rising
US folk song.
> BRIGHT MORNING STARS. US folk song, arranged by James A. Lucas.

358   Rank by Rank Again We Stand
John Huntley Skrine (1848-1923) was an Anglican cleric and educator. This text appeared in his *Thirty Hymns for Public School Singing*, 1899. It has been recast and expanded by Carl G. Seaburg. *See No. 37.*
> REUNION. Sir Henry Walford Davies (1869-1941), British composer and professor of music at University College, Aberystwyth, Wales, is presumed to be the composer of this tune. Editor of *A Students' Hymnal*, University of Wales, 1923, in which this tune first appeared, Davies was also an organist, music teacher, and conductor in Wales and England. He often attributed his compositions to the institution he served.

359   When We Are Gathered
Grace Lewis-McLaren. *See No. 73.*
REPTON. Charles Hubert Hastings Parry. *See No. 337.*

360   Here We Have Gathered
Alicia S. Carpenter. *See No. 6.*
OLD 124TH. *See No. 120.*

361   Enter, Rejoice, and Come In
Louise Ruspini (20th century). This song appears in her book *Journey to Freedom.*
REJOICE. Louise Ruspini's (20th century) tune is arranged by Betty A. Wylder. *See No. 109.*

362   Rise Up, O Flame
Anonymous.
CHALICE. Christoph Praetorius (ca. 1535-1609), born in Bunzlau, Silesia, and educated at Wittenberg University, was one of the first well-known German musicians. Praetorius wrote hymns in German and Latin and edited music textbooks. In 1563, he became cantor at Johanneim, Luneburg, and taught music until deafness forced him to retire.

363   Alleluia! Sang Stars
Mark L. Belletini. *See No. 73.*
DOXOLOGY. Patrick L. Rickey. *See No. 128.*

364   Alleluia, Alleluia
Anonymous.
BERTHIER. Jacques Berthier (1923-1994) was a composer and organist at St. Ignatius Church, Paris. From 1975 until his death he was developing a new repertoire in collaboration with Brother Roger, the founder of Taizé, an ecumenical Christian monastic community in the hills of Burgundy, France. Since its founding in 1940, visitors of all ages and backgrounds have made pilgrimages to Taizé to participate in international gatherings of prayer and reflection. Music from that religious community, such as this tune, is widely used in both Catholic and Protestant churches.

365   Praise God

Charles H. Lyttle (*see No. 290*) conceived this doxology as a bridge between theists and humanists at the height of their controversy in the late 1920s.

> DOXOLOGY. Patrick L. Rickey. *See No. 128.*

366   Heleluyan

Traditional Muskogee-Creek. This hymn, first published in *The United Methodist Hymnal*, 1989, is considered by many Creek Christians their "tribal anthem."

> HELELUYAN. Traditional Muskogee-Creek.

367   Allelu, Allelu

This hymn was originally a grace, sung before meals by Boy Scouts of America and other groups at summer camps, with the words "Praise Ye The Lord," and with singers standing only when they were singing. The origin of text and tune is unknown.

368   Now Let Us Sing

Anonymous.

> ROBESON. Anonymous. This tune was named in honor of Paul Robeson. *See No. 462.*

369   This Is the Truth That Passes Understanding

Robert Terry Weston (1898-1988) was a Unitarian Universalist minister who served churches in Nebraska, New York, Massachusetts, and Kentucky. He compiled *A Cup of Strength*, 1945, and wrote the Unitarian Universalist Association's 1963 Lenten manual, *Seasons of the Soul.*

> DONNE SECOURS. This tune was used for Psalm 12 in the 1551 edition of the Genevan Psalter, the first edition of which appeared in 1542.

370   All People That on Earth Do Dwell

William Kethe (d. ca. 1608), said to be Scottish, appeared on the Continent as a refugee from Marian persecution; he was a cleric of the Church of England for more than thirty years. The original version of this text, a paraphrase of Psalm 100, was among twenty-five of Kethe's psalm versions in the Anglo-Genevan Psalter, 1561. Alicia S. Carpenter (*see No. 6*) was commissioned to recast this text for *Singing the Living Tradition.*

> OLD HUNDREDTH. This melody was the setting for Psalm 100 in the Genevan Psalter, 1551. Although its first phrase suggests a folk

origin, it owes much to Louis Bourgeois (c. 1510-1561), Calvin's leading psalmodist. This is the original rhythm.

371   OLD HUNDREDTH. *See No. 370.* **This is the modern rhythm.**

372   TALLIS' CANON. *See No. 88.*

373   VOM HIMMEL HOCH. *See No. 110.*

374   Since what we choose is what we are
William DeWitt Hyde. This stanza concludes Hyde's hymn, "Creation's Lord, We Give Thee Thanks," 1903. The complete hymn, in revised form, appears in *Singing the Living Tradition* as No. 289.

375   As saffron trees now capture fire
Anonymous.

376   Sing loudly till the stars have heard
Anonymous.

377   In greening lands begins the song
Anonymous.

378   Let those who live in every land
Kenneth L. Patton. *See No. 303.* An earlier version of this text appears as a response in Patton's *Man Is the Meaning*, 1956.

379   Ours be the poems of all tongues
Kenneth L. Patton. *See No. 303.* This text appears as a response in Patton's *Man Is the Meaning*, 1956.

380   Rejoice in love we know and share
Charles H. Lyttle. *See No. 290.* This version of Lyttle's "Praise God" (*see No. 365*) appeared in *We Sing of Life*, 1955, revised by Edwin C. Palmer (1891-1956), Unitarian minister, and Vincent B. Silliman. *See No. 42.*

381   From all that dwell below the skies
Isaac Watts. *See No. 245.* This text combines part of the first stanza of Watts's hymn, "From All That Dwell below the Skies," with phrases from the angelic song of Luke 2:14. It appeared in *We Sing of Life*, 1955.

382   De todos bajo el cielo gran sol
This is a Spanish translation of Isaac Watts's text, "From all that dwell below the skies." *See No. 381.*

383   Alleluia Amen
Anonymous.
ALLELUIA AMEN. Anonymous.

384   Alleluia
Anonymous.
AMADEUS. Wolfgang Amadeus Mozart (1756-1791), the great Austrian composer and pianist, began writing music at age five. During his brief life, he composed more than 600 works, including operas, symphonies, church music, serenades, and chamber music.

385   Gloria
Anonymous.
JACQUES. Jacques Berthier. *See No. 364.*

386   Alleluia Chaconne
Anonymous.
PACHELBEL'S CANON. Johann Pachelbel (1653-1706) was a German composer. Organist at St. Sebalds' Church in Nuremberg, his works include many compositions for violin and for organ.

387   The Earth, Water, Fire, Air
Anonymous.
ELEMENTS. Anonymous.

388   Dona Nobis Pacem
Traditional Latin text meaning "Give us peace."
DONA NOBIS PACEM. Traditional canon.

389   Gathered Here
Philip A. Porter. *See No. 50.*
GATHERING CHANT. Philip A. Porter. *See No. 50.*

390   Gaudeamus Hodie
Anonymous. The Latin text can be translated, "Let us be joyful today."
GAUDEAMUS HODIE. Natalie Sleeth (1930-1992) was a United Methodist composer of choral music and sacred and inspirational verses.

391   Voice Still and Small
John Corrado. *See No. 7*. The second line has been changed from the original, which began, "In dark and rain, sorrow and pain."
   VOICE STILL AND SMALL. John Corrado. *See No. 7*.

392   Hineh Mah Tov
Psalm 133:1, which can be translated, "How good it is for brethren to dwell together!" This joyous song may be sung in unison or as a round.
   PSALM 133. Hebrew round.

393   Jubilate Deo
Anonymous.
   JUBILATE DEO. Michael Praetorius (1571-1621) was one of the leading composers of the middle German school of organ composition.

394   Hava Nashirah
Hebrew round.
   HAVA NASHIRAH. Hebrew round.

395   Sing and Rejoice
Traditional round.
   MOORE. Traditional round. This tune is named in honor of Christopher Moore. *See No. 249*.

396   I Know This Rose Will Open
Mary E. Grigolia (1947-), a Unitarian Universalist minister, has served the Southwest Unitarian Universalist Church of Strongsville, Ohio, and the Unitarian Universalist Fellowship in Oberlin, Ohio.
   GRIGOLIA. Mary E. Grigolia (1947-).

397   Morning Has Come
Traditional round.
   MOORE. *See No. 395*.

398   To See the World
William Blake. *See No. 17*. This text is an excerpt from *Auguries of Innocence*.
   DEN STORE HVIDE FLOK. Norwegian melody (ca. 1600) arranged by Edvard Grieg (1843-1907), a Unitarian Norwegian composer. Grieg drew on the Norwegian folk tradition to compose many memo-

rable songs, works for piano, and choral pieces. In 1867 he founded the Norwegian Academy of Music in Christiania (now Oslo).

399   Vine and Fig Tree
Arranged from Micah 4:3-4.
> VINE AND FIG TREE. Traditional Hebrew.

400   Shalom Havayreem
The Hebrew words mean "Peace, friends, until we meet again" and are used as a greeting or farewell. This song became popular in the Jewish colonies in Palestine after World War II.
> SHALOM. Southeastern European, Hebrew four-voice round. In this part of Europe, Jewish and non-Jewish folk songs are practically identical. The original mode was Dorian.

401   Kum ba Yah
African American spiritual (ca. 1750-1875). "Kum ba yah" (come by here) comes from the Gullah language, spoken in the South Carolina low country.
> DESMOND. Anonymous. The tune, named after Desmond Tutu (*see No. 593*), is harmonized by Carlton R. Young. *See No. 18.*

402   From You I Receive
Joseph and Nathan Segal (20th century) are rabbis, artists, and musicians.
> RABBI. Joseph and Nathan Segal (20th century).

403   Spirit of Truth, of Life, of Power
Horace Westwood (1884-1956), born in Yorkshire, England, was a Methodist preacher in Great Britain and the US before becoming a Unitarian minister in 1910. He subsequently served Unitarian churches in Ohio, Manitoba, and California, and was a mission preacher for the Unitarian Laymen's League. His books include *Some Hymns and Verses*.
> HAMBURG. Lowell Mason (*see No. 87*) composed this tune in Savannah, Georgia, in 1824 and published it in the third edition of the *Boston Handel and Haydn Society Collection of Church Music*.

404   What Gift Can We Bring
Jane Manton Marshall. *See No. 33.*
> ANNIVERSARY SONG. Jane Manton Marshall. *See No. 33.*

405   This Do in Memory of Me
Wayne Bradley Robinson (1936-) is the editor of *Journeys toward Narrative Preaching*, 1990. This text draws on Luke 22:19-20.
ST. BOTOLPH. Gordon Slater (1896-1979).

406   Let Us Break Bread Together
Traditional.
LET US BREAK BREAD. Traditional.

407   We're Gonna Sit at the Welcome Table
Traditional.
WELCOME TABLE. Traditional, arranged by Mary Allen Walden. *See No. 116.*

408   Wonder of Wonders
Brian Wren. *See No. 23.*
OF WONDERS. Alan Hovhaness (1911-), US composer, conductor, and teacher, studied composition and piano at the New England Conservatory of Music. He has received grants from the National Institute of Arts and Letters and the Guggenheim Foundation, among others. His work is influenced by Armenian and Eastern music. This tune was commissioned for *Singing the Living Tradition.*

409   Sleep, My Child
Traditional lullaby. Alicia S. Carpenter was commissioned to adapt this text for *Singing the Living Tradition. See No. 6.*
AR HYD Y NOS. Welsh melody (ca. 1784).

410   Surprised by Joy
Eric Routley (1917-1982), a British hymnologist, was the editor of *Rejoice in the Lord*, the hymnal of the Christian Reformed Church in America, and consultant to *The Hymnal 1982* of the Episcopal Church. This text was adapted by Joan Goodwin (1926-), Unitarian Universalist religious educator and writer. She served on the staff of the Unitarian Universalist Association in several positions, including vice president for extension and district services, and was director of religious education for the Church of the Larger Fellowship for several years. In 1972 she won the UUA's Angus H. MacLean Award for excellence in religious education.
O WALY, WALY. English folk melody, harmonized by John Weaver. *See No. 225.*

411   Part in Peace

Sarah Flower Adams. *See No. 87.*

CHARLESTON. From William Walker's *The Southern Harmony. See No. 15.* Harmonized by Alastair Cassels-Brown. *See No. 161.*

412   Let Hope and Sorrow Now Unite

Brian Wren. *See No. 23.*

ALLEIN GOTT IN DER HOH. Nikolaus Decius (ca. 1490-1541). Harmonized by Hieronymous Praetorius (ca. 1560-1629).

413   Go Now in Peace

Natalie Sleeth. *See No. 390.* The text is based on Luke 2:29.

GO IN PEACE. Natalie Sleeth. *See No. 390.*

414   As We Leave This Friendly Place

Vincent B. Silliman. *See No. 42.*

SEGNE UNS. Adapted from *Chorale 38* by Johann Sebastian Bach. *See No. 41.*

415   Hevenu Shalom Aleychem

Traditional Hebrew. The text can be translated, "We bring greetings of peace."

HEVENU. Traditional Hebrew.

Notes on Readings

416   Holy and beautiful the custom which brings us together
Robert French Leavens (1878-1961), a Unitarian minister, served churches in Massachusetts, Nebraska, and California before becoming chaplain of Mills College in Oakland, California. He was the editor of *Great Companions*, Vol. I, 1927, and, with his sister Mary Agnes Leavens, of Vol. II, 1941. This text, abridged here, is from *Let Us Pray*, 1939.

417   For the beauty of the earth
Barbara J. Pescan (1945-) is a Unitarian Universalist minister serving the Unitarian Church of Evanston, Illinois. She previously served congregations in Northern Fairfield County and West Redding, Connecticut, and Oak Park, Illinois. Before becoming a minister she worked as a counselor and probation officer.

418   Come into the circle of love and justice
Israel Zangwill (1864-1926) was an English writer and Jewish leader. These opening words are from "Jehovah" in *Blind Children*, 1903.

419   Look to this day!
This text is attributed to Kalidasa (3rd century CE), a great Indian author of epic poems and dramas. He was probably a Brahman, or Hindu priest.

420   We are here to abet creation and to witness to it
Annie Dillard (1945-), US writer, grew up in Pittsburgh, Pennsylvania. In 1975 she won the Pulitzer Prize for Nonfiction for *Pilgrim at Tinker Creek*. Her other books include works of fiction, nature writing, essays, criticism, and memoir.

421   O sing a new song to the Eternal
Psalm 98:1,4-5,7-8. From *The Holy Bible*, translated by James Moffat, 1935.

422   Surely the Lord is in this place
Genesis 28:16a, 17b. From the *New Revised Standard Version Bible*, 1989.

423   It is a joy to give thanks to the Eternal
Psalm 92. From *The Holy Bible*, translated by James Moffat, 1935.

424   Have you entered the storehouses of the snow?
Job 38:22, 29-30. From the *New Revised Standard Version Bible*, 1989, with slight alterations.

425   Thus have you prepared the land
Psalm 65:9-13. From *Psalms Anew: In Inclusive Language*, compiled by Nancy Schreck and Maureen Leach, 1986.

426   The wilderness and dry land shall be glad
Isaiah 35:1-2. From the *New Revised Standard Version Bible*, 1989.

427   Who has cut a channel for the torrents of rain
Job 38:25-27. Adapted from the *New Revised Standard Version Bible*, 1989.

428   Come out of the dark earth
May Sarton (1912-1995), a Unitarian Universalist, was a popular poet and novelist whose work examined such universal themes as love, aging, and the search for self-knowledge. Born in Wondelgem, Belgium, and brought to the United States at the age of four, her many books include novels, journals, poetry, and works for children. Among her best-known works are the novel, *Mrs. Stevens Hears the Mermaids Singing*, 1965, and her *Collected Poems, 1930-1993*, published in 1993. This reading is an excerpt from "Invocation," published in *A Grain of Mustard Seed*, 1971.

429   Come into this place of peace
William F. Schulz (1949-) was the president of the Unitarian Universalist Association from 1985 to 1993. Before joining the UUA staff, he served as minister of the First Parish Unitarian Church in Bedford, Massachusetts. He is currently executive director of Amnesty International, USA.

430   For now the winter is past
Song of Solomon 2:11-13. From the *New Revised Standard Version Bible*, 1989. The text has been abridged.

431   O Spinner, Weaver, of our lives
Barbara Wells (1960-) a Unitarian Universalist minister, founded the New Congregation Ministry of the Unitarian Universalist Church in Woodinville, Washington, in 1991. She previously served the East Shore Unitarian Church in Bellevue, Washington. This reading was written after the 1984 Women's Interseminary Conference in Chicago.

432   If someone would scatter seed on the ground
Adapted from Mark 4:26-29, in the *New Revised Standard Version Bible*,
1989.

433   How rare it is, how lovely
Adapted from Psalm 133:1 in *The Holy Bible*, translated by James Moffat,
1935.

434   May we be reminded here of our highest aspirations
Anonymous.

435   We come together this morning to remind one another
Kathleen McTigue (1956-), born in Spokane, Washington, is minister of
the Unitarian Society of New Haven in Hamden, Connecticut. She was
previously a minister of the Unitarian Universalist Fellowship Church in
Winston-Salem, North Carolina.

436   We come to this time and this place
David C. Pohl (1930-) was the Unitarian Universalist Association's director of ministry from 1979 to 1993. He has also served Unitarian Universalist churches in Bedford, Massachusetts; Cleveland, Ohio; and Ottawa,
Ontario, and in other positions with the UUA.

437   LET US WORSHIP
Kenneth L. Patton. *See No. 303.* This reading is taken from *Man Is the
Meaning*, 1956.

438   MORNING
Clinton Lee Scott (1890-1985) served Universalist churches for seventy
years in Vermont, New York, Pennsylvania, California, Georgia, Illinois,
Ohio, Massachusetts, and Florida. Superintendent of Universalist Churches
in Massachusetts and Connecticut for ten years, he received the Award for
Distinguished Service to Unitarian Universalism in 1977. His publications
include *Promise of Spring*, the 1977 Unitarian Universalist Association
Meditation Manual.

439   WE GATHER IN REVERENCE
Sophia Lyon Fahs (1876-1978) was an educator ordained into the Unitarian
ministry in 1959. A pioneer in religious education, she worked with Harry
Emerson Fosdick (*see No. 115*) at Riverside Church in New York City before becoming editor of religious education materials for the American

Unitarian Association and the Council of Liberal Churches. In 1951, she received the American Unitarian Association's Award for Distinguished Service. Among her books are *Jesus, the Carpenter's Son*, 1945; *From Long Ago and Many Lands*, 1948; and *Today's Children and Yesterday's Heritage*, 1952, from which these opening words came.

440   FROM THE FRAGMENTED WORLD
Phillip Hewett (1925-) is a Unitarian minister born in Dorchester, England. The 1992 recipient of the Award for Distinguished Service to the Cause of Unitarian Universalism, Hewett was the longtime minister of the Unitarian Church of Vancouver, British Columbia, where he is now minister emeritus.

441   TO WORSHIP
Jacob Trapp. *See No. 139.*

442   WE BID YOU WELCOME
Richard S. Gilbert. *See No. 322.*

443   WE ARRIVE OUT OF MANY SINGULAR ROOMS
Kenneth L. Patton. *See No. 303.* This reading appears in *Man Is the Meaning*, 1956.

444   THIS HOUSE
Kenneth L. Patton. *See No. 303.* This reading appears in *Man Is the Meaning*, 1956.

445   THE WOMB OF STARS
Joy Atkinson (1947-), minister of the Unitarian Universalist Church in San Mateo, California, previously served other congregations in California and Minnesota. This text was written to acknowledge and celebrate the interdependent web of existence, using maternal imagery to speak about the cosmos-source of our being.

446   TO THE FOUR DIRECTIONS
Joan Goodwin. *See No. 410.* This text was first published in *Quest*, a monthly publication of the Church of the Larger Fellowship.

447   At times our own light goes out and is rekindled
Albert Schweitzer (1875-1965) was a theologian, musician, physician, and humanitarian. In his early life, he studied philosophy and music and pub-

lished notable work on theology and the historical Jesus. Later, motivated by his ethical philosophy of "reverence for life," he became a doctor and founded, funded, and administered a hospital in Gabon, Africa, which he directed until his death. In 1952, he won the Nobel Peace Prize for his work as a physician and humanitarian. These lines are taken from Schweitzer's *Memoirs of Childhood and Youth*, 1931.

448 We gather this hour as people of faith
Christine Robinson (1952-) is a Unitarian Universalist minister. Born in Portland, Oregon, she serves the First Unitarian Church in Albuquerque, New Mexico. She previously served the Unitarian Universalist Fellowship in Columbia, South Carolina.

449 We hallow this time together by kindling the lamp of our heritage
Albert Hill Thelander (1925-) served the Humboldt Unitarian Universalist Fellowship in Bayside, California, from 1979 to 1993. Born in Jamestown, New York, he was ordained at the Unitarian Universalist Church of Saddleback Valley in Laguna Hills, California.

450 Blessed is the match consumed in kindling flame
Hannah Senesh (1921-1944), born in Budapest, Hungary, was an anti-Nazi activist known for her heroic efforts to save Jews during the German occupation of Hungary. In 1939, protesting the passing of the anti-Semitic Jewish Bill, Senesh moved to Palestine to work on a Zionist farm. When reports of injustice against the Jewish community continued, she returned to Hungary to organize Jewish resistance. In 1944, Senesh and thirty-one volunteers parachuted into Yugoslavia to start a resistance movement and were captured and tortured upon reaching Hungary. Senesh was executed by the Nazis for treason. Her journal, begun at age thirteen, was published posthumously in *Hannah Senesh: Her Life and Diary*, 1972. This reading is from *Gates of the House: The New Union Home Prayerbook*, edited by Chaim Stern (*see No. 633*), 1976.

451 Flame of fire, spark of the universe
Leslie Pohl-Kosbau (1949-), lifelong Unitarian Universalist and member of First Unitarian Church of Portland, Oregon, is an adult religious education teacher.

452 Life is a gift for which we are grateful
Marjorie Montgomery (1935-), a Unitarian Universalist minister, has served congregations in Belmont, Massachusetts, and Fort Worth and Dallas, Texas.

This reading may be followed by the following congregational response: "In the light of truth and the warmth of love, we gather to seek, to sustain, to share."

453   May the light we now kindle
From the Passover Haggadah. Passover commemorates the Israelites' escape from slavery in Egypt and their courage in finding and rebuilding their homeland. The Haggadah is the narration of the Passover story used for the home celebration of this holiday.

454   In our time of grief, we light a flame of sharing
Christine Robinson. *See No. 448.*

455   Each morning we must hold out the chalice
Dag Hammarskjöld (1905-1961), Swedish statesman, was the secretary-general of the United Nations from 1953 to 1961. He was a lifelong diplomat and spokesperson for international cooperation and economic progress. After his death in a plane crash while on a UN mission to Africa, he was posthumously awarded the Nobel Prize for Peace. This reading comes from his journal, *Markings*, published in English translation in 1964.

456   EXTINGUISHING THE CHALICE
Elizabeth Selle Jones (1926-), a Unitarian Universalist minister, served the Unitarian Universalist Church in Livermore, California, from her ordination in 1980 until her retirement. This chalice reading was written to express her desire to formalize the extinguishing of the chalice as well as its lighting to complete the ceremony, which became part of the Sunday tradition for her congregation.

457   I am only one but still I am one
Edward Everett Hale (1822-1909), a Unitarian minister, served churches in Boston and was chaplain of the United States Senate. Much of his life was devoted to the cause of international peace. He is the author of *The Man Without a Country* and numerous poems, including "The Nameless Saint."

458   Mindful of truth ever exceeding our knowledge
Walter Royal Jones Jr. (1920-), a Unitarian Universalist minister, served congregations in Gloucester, Massachusetts, and Charlottesville, Virginia, as well as the Foothills Unitarian Church, Fort Collins, Colorado, of which he is minister emeritus. He received the Award for Distinguished Service to Unitarian Universalism in 1995. This covenant grew out of a worship

workshop in the early 1960s and was used at the Independent Christian Church in Gloucester. It first appeared in *Hymns for the Celebration of Life*, 1964.

459   This is the mission of our faith
William F. Schulz. *See No. 429.*

460   The line in life, nature, science, philosophy
Sarah Alden Ripley (1793-1867), born in Boston, Massachusetts, was a noted classical scholar and teacher. She and her husband, Samuel, a Unitarian Universalist minister in Waltham, Massachusetts, taught at a Boston preparatory school for boys. Ripley's depth of knowledge in science caused her to question life after death, free will, and predestination, yet she remained a lifelong Unitarian. Many of her letters were published posthumously, including a letter to Unitarian minister George Francis Simons, from which this reading is taken.

461   WE MUST BE SAVED
Reinhold Niebuhr (1892-1971) was an ordained minister of the Evangelical Synod for North America, now part of the United Church of Christ. A crusader for social justice and ethics, he wrote numerous books and papers on societal and religious issues, which are still used in seminaries around the world. In 1964 he received the Presidential Medal of Freedom. His publications include *Moral Man and Immoral Society*, 1932; *Faith and History*, 1949; and *The Irony of American History*, 1952, from which this reading comes.

462   I shall take my voice
Paul Robeson (1898-1976) was a brilliant African American singer and actor particularly known for his portrayal of Othello. Although he was never charged, arrested, or brought to trial, Robeson was blacklisted and prevented from traveling after World War II because of his advocacy of friendship with the Soviet Union and his political work on behalf of the colonial people of Africa. In response to a member of the House UnAmerican Activities Committee who asked why he didn't move to Russia, Robeson responded, "[M]y father was a slave and my people died to build this country, and I'm going to stay right here and have a part of it just like you." This affirmation is from *The Whole World in His Hand: A Pictorial Biography of Paul Robeson* by Susan Robeson, 1981.

463 My heart is moved by all I cannot save

Adrienne Rich (1929-), US poet and essayist, was born in Baltimore. Her many awards include the National Book Award in 1974 for *Diving Into the Wreck* and a MacArthur Fellowship in 1994. She is the author of *A Wild Patience Has Taken Me This Far*, 1981; *Dark Fields of the Republic*, 1995; and many other books. These are the concluding lines from "Natural Resources," published in *The Dream of a Common Language*, 1978.

464 AND THEN

Judy Chicago (1939-), US artist and writer, has been a leading figure in the recognition of women in the arts. An assistant professor at the University of California in Los Angeles from 1969 to 1971 and founder of the Women's Art Program, she was also a cofounder of the California Institute of the Arts; the Feminist Studio Workshop in Los Angeles; Womanspace, an alternative women's art gallery; and Woman's Building, an alternative arts institution. Her works include *Through the Flower*, 1975; *The Birth Project*, 1985; and *The Dinner Party*, 1979, from which this poem comes.

465 THE WISDOM TO SURVIVE

Wendell Berry (1934-). *See No. 342.* This reading is an excerpt from "Work Song," published in *Clearing*, 1977.

466 RELIGION

Vincent B. Silliman. *See No. 42.* This reading comes from *We Speak of Life*, 1955.

467 LISTEN, ISRAEL

Deuteronomy 6:4-7. This affirmation comes from *The Holy Bible*, translated by James Moffat, 1935.

468 WE NEED ONE ANOTHER

George E. Odell. This is from *Gates of Repentance: The New Union Prayer Book*, edited by Chaim Stern, 1978. *See No. 633.*

469 THE SPIRIT OF WISDOM

Wisdom of Solomon 7:1-7, from *The New Revised Standard Version Bible*, 1989. This text has been abridged.

470 AFFIRMATION

Leonard Mason (1912-), an English Unitarian minister, has served churches in England and Canada since 1943. He is now minister emeritus of the

Unitarian Church of Montreal. This reading was included in *Bold Antiphony*, a compilation of reference materials for nontraditional worship in English Unitarian churches.

471   Love is the doctrine of this church
L. Griswold Williams (1893-1942) was a Universalist minister who served churches in Pennsylvania, Vermont, and New York. He was a member of the commission that produced *Hymns of the Spirit and Services of Religion*, 1937; he also compiled *Antiphonal Readings for Free Worship*, 1933, which included this text.

472   In the freedom of the truth
Charles Gordon Ames (1828-1912), with little formal training, became a Free Baptist home missionary in Minnesota. In 1859 he gathered the Unitarian church in Bloomington, Illinois, "the church of Lincoln's friends," and became a propagandist for Abraham Lincoln. For twenty years he served the Church of Disciples, Unitarian, in Boston. This text was devised circa 1880 as the covenant for the Spring Garden Unitarian Society, Philadelphia, which he founded.

473   Love is the spirit of this church
James Vila Blake (1842-1925), a Unitarian minister, served several congregations in Illinois. His publications include *Unity Hymns and Chorales*, 1892, edited with W. C. Gannett (*see No. 39*) and F. L. Hosmer (*see No. 45*). This reading comes from the covenant adopted by the Church of All Souls, Evanston, on April 29, 1894.

474   UNTO THE CHURCH UNIVERSAL
Keshab Chandra Sen (1838-1884) joined and became a leader in the Brahmo Samaj, a Hindu reform movement founded by Rammohun Roy (ca. 1774-1833). The Brahmo Samaj was in touch with British and American Unitarianism and devoted to the understanding of, and fellowship with, all faiths. This text was arranged by John Haynes Holmes. *See No. 82.*

475   WE, THE PEOPLES OF THE UNITED NATIONS
Abridged from the preamble of the charter of the United Nations, which was adopted in San Francisco, California, on June 26, 1945.

476   Before the wonders of life we acknowledge
Von Ogden Vogt (1879-1964) was a Unitarian minister whose description of worship as "the celebration of life" provided the title for *Hymns for the*

Celebration of Life, 1964. He served Congregational churches before settling at the First Unitarian Society of Chicago. His publications include *Art and Religion*, 1921, and *Modern Worship*, 1927. He was a member of the Unitarian and Universalist commissions that produced *Hymns of the Spirit and Services of Religion*, 1937, from which this reading comes.

477   Forgive us that often we forgive ourselves so easily
Vivian Towse Pomeroy (1883-1961) was born and educated in England, where he was ordained a Congregational minister. He served the First Congregational Parish in Milton, Massachusetts (Unitarian), from 1924 to 1961. His publications include sermons, children's books, stories, and *New Prayers in Old Places*, 1955.

478   A PRAYER OF SORROW
United Nations Environmental Sabbath Program.

479   An awe so quiet, I don't know when it began
Denise Levertov (1923-1997), born in England, was a poet. During World War II she served returning veterans as a civil rehabilitation nurse in London; she later married an American soldier, moved to the United States, and became a US citizen. She helped found the Writers and Artists Protest against the Vietnam War and was also an anti-nuclear activist. A teacher at Stanford University from 1981 to 1994, she published more than twenty volumes of poetry after 1945, including *Oblique Prayers*, 1984, from which this reading comes.

480   Let us open our minds and hearts
Composite.

481   It is our quiet time
Nancy Wood (1936-), born in Trenton, New Jersey, is a writer and photographer. She was the 1980 winner of the Carter Woodson Award from the National Council for Social Studies for *War Cry on a Prayer Feather: Prose and Poetry of the Ute Indians*. Much of her poetry and writing portrays her concern for and love of Native Americans and the environment. Her many books include *Many Winters: Prose and Poetry of the Pueblos*, 1974, and *The Serpent's Tongue: Prose, Poetry, and Art of the New Mexico Pueblos*, 1997. This poem is from *Hollering Sun*, 1972.

482   If it is language that makes us human
Jacob Trapp. *See No. 139.*

483   When despair for the world grows in me
Wendell Berry. *See No. 342.* This reading is published as "The Peace of Wild Things" in *Openings*, 1968.

484   To live content with small means
William Henry Channing (1810-1884), a Unitarian minister, was a leader in social reform movements before the Civil War. A nephew of William Ellery Channing (*see No. 592*), his contribution to Transcendentalism was his attempt to change the individualist emphasis of the movement to one that focused instead on the progress of the human race as a whole.

485   Turn scarlet, leaves!
Raymond J. Baughan (1912-1993), a Unitarian Universalist minister for fifty-five years, served Unitarian Universalist congregations in Ohio and throughout the Northeast. After retiring in 1978, he served as interim minister for ten congregations from Milwaukee to San Francisco. He was the author of many books of meditations, sermons, and poems, including *The Sound of Silence*, the Unitarian Universalist Association's 1965 Meditation Manual, and *If The Shoe Fits*, a collection of sermons, 1992. This text was created "to sing with the changing universe in which I live."

486   I am being driven forward into an unknown land
Dag Hammarskjöld. *See No. 455.*

487   The bell is full of wind
Roberto Juarroz (1925-) is an Argentinean poet. An English translation of his *Poesia vertical* was published as *Vertical Poetry*, 1976; it is the source of this reading.

488   Hold fast to dreams
Langston Hughes. *See No. 60.* "Dreams," the source of this reading, was published in *The Dream Keeper and Other Poems*, 1932.

489   When love is felt or fear is known
Max A. Coots (1927-) served the Unitarian Universalist Church in Canton, New York, for thirty-two years and is currently that congregation's minister emeritus. He also serves as minister of the First Universalist Church in Central Square, New York. He is the author of *Seasons of the Self*, 1994.

490   WILD GEESE

Mary Oliver (1935-) is a US poet whose work explores the natural landscape and fundamental questions of life and death. A longtime resident of
Provincetown, Massachusetts, she has taught creative writing at Sweet
Briar College, Bennington College, and other institutions. Her many books
of poems include *American Primitive*, 1983, winner of the Pulitzer Prize
for Poetry; *New and Selected Poems*, 1992, winner of the National Book
Award; and *Dream Works*, 1986, from which "Wild Geese" comes.

491   THE APHORISMS OF JESUS

In order, these verses are Luke 17:20-21, 12:27, 12:34, 8:16, 7:35, 6:44, 6:37,
and 6:31.

492   FRAGILE AND ROOTED

Carolyn S. Owen-Towle (1935-), a Unitarian Universalist minister, was
president of the Unitarian Universalist Ministers Association from 1989
to 1991. Since 1978 she and her husband, Thomas Owen-Towle, have been
co-ministers of the First Unitarian Church in San Diego, California. She is
the author of several collections of sermons including *Step Off the Side-
walk*, 1992.

493   Fire of the Spirit

Hildegard of Bingen. *See No. 27.* This text, a free translation by Charles
Williams (1886-1945), was published in *The Oxford Book of Prayer*, 1985,
and has been abridged here.

494   The prayer of our souls is a petition for persistence

W. E. B. Du Bois (1863-1963) was a pioneering sociologist and Black protest
leader. He helped found the National Association for the Advancement of
Colored People in 1909 and edited its magazine, *The Crisis*, from 1910 to
1934. As a scholar he published *The Philadelphia Negro*, the first socio-
logical study of a US Black community, in 1899, and taught economics and
history at Atlanta University for many years. Disillusioned by American
apathy toward the racial dilemma, he renounced his citizenship and exiled
himself to Ghana in 1961, where he died. His publications include *The
Souls of Black Folk*, 1903; *Black Reconstruction*, 1935; and *The Autobiography of W. E. B. Du Bois*, 1968. This prayer, written in 1909 or 1910, was
published in *Prayers for Dark People*, 1980.

495   Hear me, four quarters of the world

Black Elk (Nicholas Black Elk) (1863-1950), second cousin of Crazy Horse, was an Oglala Sioux holy man. He witnessed the 1876 victory of Sioux warriors over George A. Custer at the Battle of Little Big Horn and the 1890 massacre of the Lakota Sioux at the Wounded Knee encampment. As a young man he began to have visions of his ancestral grandfathers; he shared some of them in *Black Elk Speaks*, as told to John G. Neihardt, 1932. This reading comes from Chapter 1.

496   From arrogance, pompousness
Harry Meserve (1914-) is a Unitarian Universalist minister. He served churches for forty years in Massachusetts, New York, California, Michigan, and Ellsworth, Maine, where he is minister emeritus. He was also a member of the executive staff of the Rockefeller Foundation from 1957 to 1960, and director of programs and editor of the *Journal of Religion and Health* at the Academy of Religion and Mental Health from 1960 to 1965.

497   Prayer invites God to be present
Abraham J. Heschel (1907-1972), born in Warsaw, Poland, was a major Jewish theologian and philosopher. Following the outbreak of World War II, he emigrated first to England and then to the United States. From 1943 until his death, he taught philosophy, ethics, and mysticism at the Jewish Theological Seminary of America in New York. He was also an activist for civil rights and worked with the Institute of Non-Violent Social Change. Heschel's major works, including *Man Is Not Alone*, 1951; *God in Search of Man*, 1956; and *A Passion for Truth*, 1973, concern the relationship between the people and God. This reading has been adapted from *Gates of Prayer: The New Union Prayerbook*, 1975.

498   In the quietness of this place
Howard Thurman (1899-1981) was a beloved minister, philosopher, and educator. He served as professor of theology at Howard University and dean of its Rankin Chapel; cofounder and minister of the interdenominational, interracial Church for the Fellowship of All People in San Francisco; dean of Marsh Chapel at Boston University; and member of the Unitarian Universalist Commission on Race. His books, including *Jesus and the Disinherited*, 1949; *Meditations of the Heart*, 1953; and *Disciplines of the Spirit*, 1963, are widely read.

499   And I have felt a presence
William Wordsworth. *See No. 333.* This reading is an excerpt from "Lines Composed a Few Miles Above Tintern Abbey," 1798.

500   Marvelous truth, confront us at every turn

Denise Levertov. *See No. 479.* This reading is an excerpt from "Matins," published in *The Jacob's Ladder,* 1961.

501   Spirit of Community, in which we share and find strength

Frederick E. Gillis (1940-), a Unitarian Universalist minister, serves the Westminster Unitarian Church, East Greenwich, Rhode Island. Previously he served congregations in Rockland, Massachusetts, and Halifax, Nova Scotia.

502   Now is the accepted time

W. E. B. Du Bois. *See No. 494.* This prayer, written in 1909 or 1910, appears in *Prayers for Dark People,* 1980.

503   Bless Adonai who spins day into dusk

Rami M. Shapiro (1951-), a rabbi and peace activist, has served Temple Beth Or in Miami, Florida, since 1981. His many books include *Wisdom of the Jewish Sages,* 1995, and *Minyan,* 1997.

504   i thank You God for most this amazing day

e. e. cummings. *See No. 250.* This poem, from *XAIPE,* 1950, appears in its entirety.

505   Let us be at peace with our bodies and our minds

Thich N'hat Hanh is a Zen Buddhist monk, poet, and teacher. He was chair of the Vietnamese Buddhist peace delegation during the Vietnam War, and in 1967, Martin Luther King Jr. nominated him for the Nobel Peace Prize. His published works include *The Miracle of Mindfulness,* 1976; *Being Peace,* 1987; and *Living Buddha, Living Christ,* 1995. This reading is taken from *Being Peace.*

506   May the glory of the passing away of autumn

Barbara J. Pescan. *See No. 417.*

507   Grant us the ability to find joy and strength

Jewish prayer. From the United Nations Environmental Sabbath Program resources.

508   Save us from weak resignation to violence

Christian prayer. From the United Nations Environmental Sabbath Program resources.

509   Save us, our compassionate Lord
Muslim prayer. From the United Nations Environmental Sabbath Program resources.

510   O Spirit of Life and Renewal
Jane Rzepka (1950-), a Unitarian Universalist minister, was born in Cleveland, Ohio. Minister of the Unitarian Universalist Church in Reading, Massachusetts, she previously served as assistant minister of the Unitarian Society in Winchester, Massachusetts. She is the author of *A Small Heaven*, the 1989 Unitarian Universalist Association Meditation Manual.

511   Let there be peace in the sky
Atharva Veda (ca. 400 BCE). The vedas—collections of hymns, rituals, and commentaries—are the primary scriptures for many traditions of Hinduism.

512   WE GIVE THANKS THIS DAY
O. Eugene Pickett (1925-), president of the Unitarian Universalist Association from 1979 to 1985, was born in Winfield, Maryland. The 1989 recipient of the Award for Distinguished Service to the Cause of Unitarian Universalism, he and his wife, Helen Pickett (*see No. 309*), also received the International Association for Religious Freedom, US Chapter Award for their contribution to creating a greater understanding between people of diverse religious and racial backgrounds. Before and after his term as UUA president, Pickett served congregations in Richmond, Virginia; Atlanta, Georgia; and Boston, Massachusetts, and worked for the Unitarian Universalist Association's Department of Ministry. This litany was written for an ecumenical worship service as part of a national reproductive rights rally in Washington, DC.

513   Our Father in heaven
Matthew 6:9-13. Known to Christians as the Lord's Prayer, this version is adapted from the *New Revised Standard Version Bible*, 1989.

514   God, lover of us all
Lala Winkley (20th century) is a British writer. This prayer was first delivered at "Widening the Web," Indigo Gate, Greenham Common, December 1985.

515 WE LIFT UP OUR HEARTS IN THANKS
Richard M. Fewkes (1936-) is a Unitarian Universalist minister who has
served the First Parish Unitarian Church in Norwell, Massachusetts, since
1969. Previously, he was the minister at the First Unitarian Universalist
Society in Middleboro, Massachusetts. He has also taught at the Andover
Newton Theological School in Newton, Massachusetts, which he attended.

516 O God, root and source of body and soul
Khasi Unitarian prayer. The Unitarian Union of the Khasi Hills in North-
eastern India, founded in 1887 by a native tribesman who was exposed to
American Unitarian thought, includes several thousand members in 76
congregations. In harmony with the Khasi matrilineal society, the Khasis
worship God as the Father and the Mother.

517 I who am the beauty of the green earth
Starhawk (born Miriam Simos) (1951-) is a writer, activist, and self-pro-
claimed witch. A founding member of Reclaiming: A Center for Feminist
Spirituality and Counseling in San Francisco, she is the author of two nov-
els as well as several books on goddess spirituality, including *The Spiral
Dance*, 1979, and *Dreaming the Dark*, 1982. This reading is taken from
The Spiral Dance.

518 Grandfather, look at our brokenness
From the Ojibway (Ojibwa), also known as Chippewa or Saulteaux. The
Ojibway originated in what is now Sault Ste. Marie in the central Great
Lakes region. Between the late sixteenth and mid-nineteenth centuries the
Ojibway, traditionally dependent on hunting, trapping, and fishing, became
profitable fur traders with the French and spread their territory west into
Lake Superior and Minnesota, driving the Dakota from their homelands.

519 Let me not pray to be sheltered from dangers
Rabindranath Tagore. *See No. 185.* This reading is poem 89 in *Fruit-Gath-
ering*, 1916.

520 O our Mother the Earth
From the Tewa Indians of the southwestern United States. According to
legend, the Tewa tribe emerged from Sandy Place Lake far to the north and
discovered the sacred mountains. They were then divided into summer
and winter people and migrated down both sides of the Rio Grande, making 123 stops before being reunited into a single community.

521   May I be no one's enemy
Eusebius quoted by Stobaeus, a fifth-century anthologist of Greek authors. Of this passage, its translator Gilbert Murray (1866-1957) noted that "in the whole there is no petition for any material blessing, and, most strikingly of all, it is addressed to no personal God. It is pure prayer." Murray was a noted translator of Greek plays, professor of Greek at Oxford, and a devoted worker for peace and the League of Nations. Here, some omissions in Murray's translation, from *Five Stages of Greek Religion*, 1923, have been made.

522   Can any of you by worrying add a single hour to your span of life?
In order, these verses are Luke 12:25, 12:56, 6:41, and 9:25, as found in the *New Revised Standard Version Bible*, 1989.

523   Thou art the path
Though its thought and phrasing resemble the *Bhagavad-Gita*, we have not been able to locate the origin of this Indian text.

524   Earth mother, star mother
Starhawk. *See No. 517.* This prayer is from *The Spiral Dance.*

525   WEB
Denise Levertov. *See No. 479.* This poem was published in *A Door in the Hive*, 1989.

526   TREMBLING WITH JOY
Inuit Shaman Uvanuk (mid-19th century) was a Netsiliki Eskimo who used songs for healing. It is said that while out one winter's night, Uvanuk was hit by a fireball that lit up her internal organs. In pain and delirium she stumbled back to her village and fell down in song. The music emanated from the shaman and reportedly cleansed her and those around her with joy. From then on, she was able to heal the sick with her song. This reading can be found in *The Enlightened Heart*, 1989, edited by Stephen Mitchell. *See No. 669.*

527   IMMORTALITY
Richard Jeffries (1848-1887) was an English naturalist and writer. His published works include books for children, essays, and novels, including *Dewy Morn*, 1884, and *Amaryllis at the Fair*, 1887.

528   I'VE KNOWN RIVERS
Langston Hughes. *See No. 60.* From "The Negro Speaks of Rivers" in *Selected Poems of Langston Hughes*, 1974.

529   THE STREAM OF LIFE
Rabindranath Tagore. *See No. 185.* This reading is poem 69 in *Gitanjali*.

530   OUT OF THE STARS
Robert Terry Weston. *See No. 369.*

531   THE OVERSOUL
Ralph Waldo Emerson. *See No. 44.* In this reading from "The Over-Soul," 1841, some alterations have been made.

532   THE MUSIC OF THE SPHERES
Ernesto Cardenal (1925-) is a Nicaraguan Roman Catholic priest and poet. A former Nicaraguan minister of culture, Cardenal is a spokesperson for justice in Latin America and uses his poetry to promote Christian and Marxist reform. His works published in English include *Zero Hour and Other Documentary Poems*, 1960; *The Psalms of Struggle and Liberation*, 1972; and *Cosmic Canticle*, 1983.

533   COMFORT MY PEOPLE
Isaiah 40:1-2a, 3-4, 6, 8. The Second Isaiah announces (ca. 450 BCE) the end of the Jewish exile in Babylonia. This version is from the *New Revised Standard Version Bible*, 1989.

534   GLORIA!
Barbara J. Pescan. *See No. 417.*

535   DEEP CALLS TO DEEP
Psalm 42:1-4, 6-7, 11. From the *New Revised Standard Version Bible*, 1989.

536   MORNING POEM
Mary Oliver. *See No. 490.* "Morning Poem," reprinted here in its entirety, was published in *Dream Work*, 1986.

537   OUR WHOLE SYSTEM
Maria Mitchell (1818-1889), the first American woman astronomer, was born and raised a Quaker. She became a Unitarian as a young woman to explore spiritual and universal questions in what she felt was a more open

and freethinking environment. In 1847 she discovered a new comet, and in 1865 became the first professor of astronomy at Vassar College, where she taught until 1888. She was the first woman elected to the American Academy of Arts and Sciences.

538 HARBINGERS OF FROST
Robert T. Weston. *See No. 369.*

539 LATE OCTOBER
Maya Angelou (born Marguerite Johnson) (1928-) is a poet and performer. Widely known for her twenty-one nation tour as Bess in "Porgy and Bess," Angelou was nominated for a Tony Award for her Broadway debut in "Look Away." Her many literary works include *I Know Why the Caged Bird Sings*, 1970; *And Still I Rise*, 1978; and *All God's Children Need Traveling Shoes*, 1986. This reading is from *Just Give Me a Cool Drink of Water 'fore I Diiie*, 1981.

540 THE PEACE OF AUTUMN
Rabindranath Tagore. *See No. 185.*

541 WINTER MEDITATION
Denise Levertov. *See No. 479.* This poem appears as "Envy" in *A Door in the Hive*, 1989.

542 SOLSTICE
Diane Lee Moomey (1948-), writer and artist, is the author of *While on the Way Home*, 1988.

543 WINTER
Greta Crosby (1931-) is a retired Unitarian Universalist minister who served churches in Lynchburg and Roanoke, Virginia; Yakima, Washington; and Wichita, Kansas. Now minister emerita at First Unitarian Church in Wichita, she is the editor of *Tree and Jubilee*, the 1983 Unitarian Universalist Association Meditation Manual.

544 NEW YEAR'S DAY
Kathleen McTigue. *See No. 435.*

545 IN TIME OF SILVER RAIN
Langston Hughes. *See No. 60.* The poem "In Time of Silver Rain" appears in *Selected Poems of Langston Hughes*, 1974. This text has been edited.

546 TO FREE THE HEART
Francis C. Anderson Jr. (1922-) is a retired Unitarian Universalist minister who served congregations in Abington and Braintree, Massachusetts, and Savannah, Georgia.

547 SUMMER MEDITATION
Robert T. Weston. *See No. 369.*

548 SUMMER WARMTH
Helen Cohen (1943-), a Unitarian Universalist minister, is the longtime minister of the First Parish Unitarian Church in Lexington, Massachusetts. This reading is included in *Exaltation*, the 1988 UUA Meditation Manual.

549 HYMN TO MATTER
Pierre Teilhard de Chardin (1881-1955), a French philosopher and paleontologist, was a major voice in twentieth-century Christianity. A Jesuit priest, Chardin was banned from teaching and from publishing because of his view that evolution could be compatible with Christianity. The posthumous publication of his work won international attention. This reading comes from *Hymn of the Universe*, 1961.

550 WE BELONG TO THE EARTH
Attributed to Chief Noah Sealth (Chief Seattle) (1786-1866), a Native American leader. As chief of the Duwamish, Squamish, and other Native American tribes, he signed the 1855 treaty of Point Elliott, which furnished land to settlers. He had a policy of friendship with the early settlers, and Seattle, Washington, is named for him. This text has been adapted from one version of his words in a letter sent to Washington, DC.

551 EARTH TEACH ME
From the Ute Indians, who once populated the mountains and plains of present-day Colorado, Utah, Wyoming, and northern New Mexico. Utah is named for this tribe, which is now known by its three major reservations: the White River Utes of Wyoming and northwestern Colorado, the Uinta of eastern Utah, and the Uncompahgre of central Colorado. Governed by tribal councils elected by popular vote, the Ute were hunters and gatherers who developed an advanced economy by trading with the Pueblos and Spaniards.

552   MY HELP IS IN THE MOUNTAIN
Nancy Wood. *See No. 481.* This reading is from *Hollering Sun*, 1972.

553   Earth cure me
Nancy Wood. *See No. 481.* From *Hollering Sun*, 1972.

554   Water flows from high in the mountains
Thich N'hat Hanh. *See No. 505.* This text comes from *Present Moment, Wonderful Moment*, 1990.

555   SOME THINGS WILL NEVER CHANGE
Thomas Wolfe (1900-1938) was a novelist and playwright born in Asheville, North Carolina. Living for most of his life in New York City, Wolfe was the author of more than thirty plays, novels, and novella, poetry, and essay collections. He is best known for his first novel, *Look Homeward, Angel*, 1929. This text, arranged from *The Web and the Rock*, 1939, was published in *A Stone, a Leaf, a Door: Poems by Thomas Wolfe*, edited by John S. Barnes, 1945.

556   THESE ROSES
Ralph Waldo Emerson. *See No. 44.* These lines are taken from "Self-Reliance," 1841.

557   A COMMON DESTINY
David H. Eaton (1932-1992) became a Unitarian Universalist minister after serving Methodist churches for thirteen years. Prior to his death, he served the All Souls Church, Unitarian, in Washington, DC, for more than twenty years. He was the 1986 recipient of the Clarence R. Skinner Award for a sermon that best expressed Universalism's social principles and the 1992 recipient of the Holmes-Weatherly Award in recognition of his work for equality and fairness for all members of society. This meditation was written for a Sunday service.

558   FOR EVERYTHING A SEASON
Ecclesiastes 3:1-8. This version is from the *New Revised Standard Version Bible*, 1989.

559   Some day, men and women will rise
Emma Goldman (1869-1940) was a Lithuanian-born American anarchist. Having emigrated to the United States in 1885, Goldman organized stirring protests against government, abusive employers, and poverty and for

birth control and women's rights. She spent a year in prison for inciting a riot in New York City and two years for obstructing the military draft. She was finally deported to Russia in 1919. She is the author of *My Disillusionment in Russia*, 1923; *Living My Life*, 1931; and many other books on anarchism, feminism, and birth control.

560   COMMITMENT
Dorothy Day (1897-1980), US activist and writer, was the founder of the Catholic Workers movement. A convert from agnosticism to Catholicism, Day took literally the phrase from the Bible "Go, sell what you have and give to the poor." Arrested twelve times for protesting government policy toward labor, she and Peter Maurin, a French philosopher and priest, founded the *Catholic Worker* and used the monthly newspaper as a medium for worker expression.

561   Never doubt that a small group of thoughtful, committed citizens
Margaret Mead (1901-1978) was a US anthropologist who spent more than twenty years doing fieldwork in Nebraska, Samoa, New Guinea, and Bali. Her writings, popular and influential, include *Coming of Age in Samoa*, 1928; *Growing Up in New Guinea*, 1930; and *Growth and Culture*, 1951.

562   A LIFELONG SHARING
Mother Teresa (born Agnes Gonxha Bojaxhiu) (1910-1997) won the 1979 Nobel Peace Prize for her efforts to end world hunger and promote world peace. Born in Skopje, Yugoslavia, she joined the Sisters of Loreto of the Roman Catholic Church in 1928 and founded Missionaries of Charity in Calcutta in 1950, where she served for forty years. Her books include *Words to Love By*, 1983, from which this reading comes.

563   A person will worship something
Ralph Waldo Emerson. *See No. 44.*

564   LOVE IS NOT CONCERNED
Alice Walker (1944-) is an author and poet best known for her Pulitzer Prize-winning novel, *The Color Purple*, 1982. She was cofounder and publisher of Wild Trees Press in Navarro, California, and has taught at many US colleges and universities. The author of many novels, short story collections, and poems, Walker's other books include *Her Blue Body Everything We Know: Earthling Poems 1965-1990*, 1993, and *Anything We Love Can Be Saved: A Writer's Activism*, 1997. "Love Is Not Concerned" was published in *Horses Make a Landscape More Beautiful*, 1984.

565 PROPHETS
Clinton Lee Scott. *See No. 438.*

566 GOD IS ONE
Francis Dávid. *See No. 37.* Adapted by Richard Fewkes. *See No. 515.*

567 TO BE OF USE
Marge Piercy (1936-), US poet and novelist, was born in Detroit, Michigan. She is the author of more than thirty books, including the novel *He, She, and It*, 1991, and the poetry collection *Available Light*, 1988. In 1982 she published *Circles on the Water: Selected Poems of Marge Piercy*, in which "To be of use," excerpted here, appears.

568 CONNECTIONS ARE MADE SLOWLY
Marge Piercy. *See No. 567.* This reading is an excerpt from "The seven of pentacles," published in *Circles on the Water*, 1982.

569 STAND BY THIS FAITH
Olympia Brown (1835-1926) was a Universalist minister, activist, and prolific writer. The first woman officially ordained by the Universalists, she was active in the women's suffrage and temperance movements. Excerpts from her many speeches, sermons, and articles have been reprinted in *Suffrage and Religious Principle: Speeches and Writings of Olympia Brown*, edited by Dana Greene, 1983.

570 PRAYER FOR THE EARTH
Barbara Deming (1917-1984) described herself as "radical, pacifist, lesbian, feminist." She was actively involved with the Committee for Nonviolent Action in the civil rights and antiwar movements. She published books of poetry, fiction, and nonfiction, including *Prison Notes of an Anti-War Activist*, 1966. This prayer is reprinted from *Thinking Like a Mountain*, edited by John Seed, Joanna Macy, and others, 1988.

571 UNIVERSAL MINISTRY
Isaiah 61:1-4, 6. From the *New Revised Standard Version Bible*, 1989. This text has been abridged.

572 WHAT IS REQUIRED
Micah 6:6-8. From *The Holy Bible*, translated by James Moffat, 1935.

573   MOTHER'S DAY PROCLAMATION
Julia Ward Howe (1819-1910) was an author and social reformer. Best known as the author of the unofficial Union army song, "The Battle Hymn of the Republic," she used writings and lectures to promote abolition, women's rights, prison reform, and international peace. Her poetry was published in *Passion Flowers*, 1854, and other collections.

574   THE GLORIES OF PEACE
Micah 4:3-4, from the *New Revised Standard Version Bible*, 1989. The text has been abridged.

575   A NEW MANIFESTATION
Margaret Fuller (1810-1850) was a feminist writer and Transcendentalist. From 1840 to 1842 she was the editor of the Transcendentalist journal *The Dial*. In 1845 she published *Women in the Nineteenth Century*, an impassioned argument for the political equality of women. Later she became America's first woman foreign correspondent, writing for Horace Greeley's *New York Tribune*.

576   A LITANY OF RESTORATION
Marjorie Bowens-Wheatley (1949-) is a Unitarian Universalist minister serving the Community Church of New York, New York. Previously, she worked as a television producer of public affairs programs and documentaries and in a variety of positions in Unitarian Universalist organizations. This text was part of a keynote speech celebrating the 1987 founding of the Church of the Restoration in Tulsa, Oklahoma.

577   IT IS POSSIBLE TO LIVE IN PEACE
Mohandas Karamchand Gandhi (1869-1948) was the leader of India's movement for national independence. His principles of passive resistance have been used around the world by leaders such as Martin Luther King Jr. in the struggle against oppression and injustice. Gandhi entered Indian politics in 1919 and emerged as the leader of the Indian National Congress. Imprisoned for most of World War II for protesting British-imposed taxes, he was invited in 1947 to negotiate for an autonomous Indian state. He was assassinated in 1948.

578   THIS GREAT LESSON
Olympia Brown. *See No. 569.*

579 THE LIMITS OF TYRANTS
Frederick Douglass (ca. 1817-1895) was a leading African American orator and abolitionist. Born into slavery, Douglass escaped to New York in 1838 after a violent confrontation with one of his owners. Eventually, after two years in Great Britain, he purchased his freedom. He lectured widely on abolition and was the founder and editor of *The North Star*, a weekly abolitionist newspaper. His books include *Narrative of the Life of Frederick Douglass, an American Slave*, 1845, and *the Life and Times of Frederick Douglass*, 1881, from which this reading comes.

580 THE TASK OF THE RELIGIOUS COMMUNITY
Mark Morrison-Reed (1949-) is co-minister with his wife, Donna K. Morrison-Reed, of the First Unitarian Congregation of Toronto. Previously, they served as co-ministers of the First Universalist Church in Rochester, New York. A founding member of the African American Unitarian Universalist Ministry, Morrison-Reed is the co-editor, with Jacqui James, of *Been in the Storm So Long*, the Unitarian Universalist Association's 1991 Meditation Manual, and the author of *Black Pioneers in a White Denomination*, 1984, from which this reading comes.

581 PRAYER FOR HIROSHIMA DAY
James Kirkup (1927-) is a British poet and writer. He divides his time between England, the United States, and Japan, and has taught at many universities there. He is the author, editor, or translator of more than one hundred books, including fiction, travel writing, poems, plays, and works for children. His books of poetry include *Refusal to Conform: Last and First Poems*, 1963.

582 THE DIVINE JUSTICE
Amos 5:21-24 (ca. 760 BCE). This text, from the *New Revised Standard Version Bible*, 1989, has been abridged.

583 THE YOUNG DEAD SOLDIERS
Archibald MacLeish (1892-1982) was an American poet, World War I soldier, and public servant. From 1939 to 1944, he served as Librarian of Congress, and his poems often reflected his concern for democracy. MacLeish retired in 1962 after a dozen years as Boylston Professor of Rhetoric and Oratory at Harvard. He won the Pulitzer Prize for Poetry in 1933 for *Conquistador* and in 1953 for *Collected Poems*. This text is taken from *Act Five and Other Poems*, 1948.

584   A NETWORK OF MUTUALITY

Martin Luther King Jr. (1929-1968), leader of the 1960s civil rights movement, was instrumental in abolishing legal segregation in the South. As
head of the Southern Christian Leadership Conference, he promoted non-
violent resistance to oppression and was awarded the Nobel Peace Prize in
1964. King was assassinated by James Earl Ray in 1968. This reading consists of quotations from the following speeches, articles, and books: "The
American Dream," 1961; *Letter from a Birmingham City Jail*, 1963; "The
Current Crisis in Race Relations," 1958; *The Strength to Love*, 1963; the
Nobel Prize Acceptance Speech, 1964; *Where Do We Go from Here?*, 1967;
"A Christmas Sermon on Peace," 1967; and "I Have a Dream," 1963.

585   COUNCILS

Marge Piercy. *See No. 567.* This reading is an excerpt from "Councils,"
published in *Circles on the Water: Selected Poems of Marge Piercy*, 1982.

586   THE IDEA OF DEMOCRACY

Abraham Lincoln (1809-1865), the sixteenth president of the United States,
was born in Kentucky and became a lawyer in Illinois. He was elected to
the presidency in 1860. On September 22, 1862, he issued the Emancipation Proclamation. Lincoln was assassinated during his second presidential term. Lincoln spoke these words at Edwardsville, Illinois, in 1858 and
at his second inauguration in 1865.

587   A LITANY FOR SURVIVAL

Audre Lorde (1934-1992) was a US poet, essayist, and activist for feminism
and civil rights. A member of the Harlem Writers Guild, she lectured
throughout the United States and taught English at John Jay College of
Criminal Justice and Hunter College of the City University of New York.
Her major works include *The Cancer Journals*, 1980, an early account of
her battle with the disease; the novel *Zami: A New Spelling of My Name*,
1982; and *Sister Outsider: Essays and Speeches*, 1984. This reading is
adapted from her best-known collection of poems, *The Black Unicorn*, 1978.

588   TO LOOSE THE FETTERS OF INJUSTICE

Isaiah 58:6-11, abridged. From the *New Revised Standard Version Bible*,
1989.

589   PEACE

Pupils from the Lincoln School, New York, New York. This text appeared in *Creative Expression*, 1932, by Gertrude Hartman and Ann Shumaker and was arranged for *We Speak of Life*, 1955.

590   PSALM 126
Daniel Berrigan (1921-) is a Jesuit priest, activist, and poet. In the 1970s, wanted for actions against the Vietnam War at Catonsville, Maryland, he was forced underground, where he wrote the play, *Trial of the Catonsville Nine*, 1970. His numerous other books include an autobiography, *To Dwell in Peace*, 1987, and *Uncommon Prayer: A Book of Psalms*, 1978, from which this reading is taken.

591   I CALL THAT CHURCH FREE
James Luther Adams (1901-1994) was a Unitarian minister who helped to shape American religious ethics in the twentieth century. He was the recipient of the 1973 Unitarian Universalist Association's Award for Distinguished Service, the 1968 Holmes-Weatherly Award, the 1976 International Association for Religious Freedom's US Chapter Award for his contributions in expanding the understanding between people of different races and religious backgrounds, and the 1977 Melcher Book Award for his book of essays, *On Being Human Religiously*, 1976. A longtime professor at the Harvard Divinity School, he wrote several other books, including an autobiography, *Not without Dust and Heat*, published posthumously in 1995.

592   THE FREE MIND
William Ellery Channing (1780-1842), a Unitarian minister who was raised a Congregationalist, served the Federal Street Church (now the Arlington Street Church) in Boston from 1803 to 1842. His 1819 "Baltimore Sermon" on "Unitarian Christianity" polarized New England Congregational churches, creating a schism that resulted in the formation of the Unitarian denomination. This text is from the sermon "Spiritual Freedom," preached before the governor and legislature of Massachusetts in 1830. It was arranged in *We Speak of Life*, 1955.

593   LIBERATION IS COSTLY
Desmond Mpilo Tutu (1931-), winner of the 1984 Nobel Peace Prize, was a leading force in the dismantling of apartheid in South Africa. He became an Anglican parish priest in 1960 and in subsequent years became bishop of Lesotho, the first Black bishop of Johannesburg, archbishop of Cape Town, and the leader of the Anglican church in South Africa. This text is taken from *Hope and Suffering*, 1983.

594   PRINCIPLES AND PURPOSES FOR ALL OF US
Adapted from the Unitarian Universalist Association's Principles and Purposes by Helena Chapin and Mary Ann Moore for use in *Beginning Unitarian Universalism*, a religious education curriculum.

595   FREE FROM SUFFERING
Bodhisattva Vows (550 BCE), adapted. In Mahayana Buddhism, one of contemporary Buddhism's two main branches, a bodhisattva is a person who is on the path to enlightenment but vows to refrain from entering nirvana in order to assist other sentient beings to do so. The actual vows are not published.

596   BOUNDLESS GOODWILL
Metta Sutta (200 BCE) is a teaching attributed to Gautama Buddha (*see No. 184*) about the value of loving kindness toward oneself and others. Metta signifies "loving kindness," and Sutta "discourse by Buddha."

597   LOVE VERSUS HATE
Dhammapada 17, 18. This compendium of Buddha's teachings (*see No. 184*) is part of the *Sutta Pitaka* and was in existence during the reign of Asoka, emperor of India, ca. 250 BCE.

598   WITHOUT HATE
Attributed to Gautama Buddha. *See No. 184.* Based on a translation by Robert C. Childers (1838-1876), an English Orientalist, of the "Khuddaka Patha" in the *Fifth Nikaya*.

599   Why do you go to the forest in search of the Divine?
Tegh Bahadur (17th century) was a Sikh guru. Sikhs are members of one of the youngest Indian religions whose name, derived from two languages, means "disciple." Sikhism was founded by Guru Nanak (1469-1539) and draws on both Hindu and Moslem elements. Tegh Bahadur, ninth of ten of the devotional teachers, ruled from 1666 to 1675, when he was executed by the Mogul emperor Aurangzeb.

600   THE SPACE WITHIN
Lao-Tse (Lao-tzu) (5th century BCE) was the legendary founder of Taoism, one of China's major religions. According to tradition, Lao lived eighty years in the land of Chao, but then felt compelled to leave because of societal and moral decline. When he reached the border, a guard asked him if he would teach him how to live, and Lao thus wrote the book of Tao. This

text is excerpted from Chapter 11 of the *Tao Te Ching* or, in English translation, *The Way of Life.*

601   WHEN ALL THE PEOPLE
Mo-Tse (463-401 BCE) was a Chinese philosopher and international peacemaker whose vision of "universal love" is the basis of the religion known as Mohism. An anti-Confucian, Mo-Tse felt that too much emphasis was placed on the code of rituals and too little on religious teachings. Drawn to common people and simple living, he traveled throughout the western hemisphere to prevent war. The *Mo-tsu* is his principal work and contains his political, ethical, and religious teachings.

602   IF THERE IS TO BE PEACE
Lao-Tse. *See No. 600.*

603   BEYOND WORDS
Lao-Tse. *See No. 600.* This text is an adaptation of Chapter 1 of the *Tao Te Ching.*

604   A VESSEL SO SACRED
Lao-Tse. *See No. 600.* This text is Chapter 29 of the *Tao Te Ching.*

605   Oh, how great is the divine moral law
Chung Yung, also spelled *Zhong Yong*, is one of four Confucian texts published in 1190 by Chu Hsi, a neo-Confucian philosopher. It promotes the goal of moderation in all things.

606   THE TAO
From the *Tao Te Ching*, Chapter 25, attributed to Lao-Tse. *See No. 600.* This translation, by Witter Bynner (1881-1968) is titled *The Way of Life*, 1944.

607   BELOVED PRESENCE
Shams Ud-Dun Mohammad Hafiz (Shams od-Din Mohammad Hafez) (ca. 1325-1389) was a Persian lyric poet. A teacher of the Koran, he was bestowed with the title "Hafez," designated to one who has learned the Koran by heart. He lived in the tradition of Sufism, the Islamic mystical movement whose adherents are devoted to the pursuit of union with ultimate reality. Hafiz is most famous for the *Divan*, translated by H. Wilberforce Clarke (1840-1905), 1891.

608   THIS CLAY JUG
Kabir (1440-1518) was an Indian mystic, master poet, and weaver. Kabir, meaning "great one" in Arabic, was the son of a Muslim weaver in Benares. He was spiritually influenced by Sufi poets and Hindu idealism. Although he was illiterate, his works were passed on orally in Hindi and have continued to be taught through song. Some of his poems were translated by Rabindranath Tagore (*see No. 185*) in *Songs of Kabir* and by contemporary US poet Robert Bly in *The Kabir Book*, from which this text comes.

609   TO SERVE THE PEOPLE
Saadi (ca. 1184-1292), one of the greatest figures of Persian ethical and humanitarian literature, lived during the troubled period of the Mongol rule and the fall of Baghdad. He was educated in Sharaz and Baghdad, and was taught by the great mystics and scholars of his time. He later founded a school in Shiraz where he taught his disciples the mystical discipline of Sufism. This text comes from *Bostan*, a book of poems in ten chapters on ethical and mystical subjects presented through anecdotes.

610   THE JOURNEY OF LOVE
Mohammed Iqbal (1873-1938), the "spiritual founder" of Pakistan, was an Indian poet, philosopher, and political leader. Educated in philosophy, languages, and law, he lectured in history and philosophy at Government College. His poetry, based on the teachings in the Koran and the writings of eastern mystics, promoted religious, social, and political reform, including the establishment of a separate Muslim state in India. He was knighted in 1922. His principal works, written and published in Persian, Urdu, and English, include *Asrar-e khudi*, 1915, translated as *The Secrets of the Self*, 1920, 1940; *Payam-e Mashrig (The Message of the East)*, 1923; and *The Reconstruction of Religious Thought in Islam*, 1934.

611   BRAHMAN
The *Bhagavad-Gita* (500-200 BCE) is one of the most important sacred texts of Hinduism. Part of the epic *Mahabharata*, the title means "The Song of God." This text is arranged from Chapter 10 of a 1944 translation by Swami Prabhavananda, senior minister of the Vedanta Society of Southern California, and Christopher Isherwood (1904-1986), an English-born playwright and novelist, who emigrated to the United States and was a student of Vedanta, or Hindu philosophy.

612   FEARFUL JOY
Rabindranath Tagore. *See No. 185*. This reading is poem 70 in *Gitanjali*.

613   You could have golden treasure
The Upanishads are a group of more than 100 texts central to Hindu religion and philosophy. Containing stories, poems, and teachings, they deal with the relationship of the universal soul to the individual. The Chandogya is believed to be among the oldest Upanishads, probably written between 900 and 600 BCE.

614   THE SACRED HOOP
Black Elk. *See No. 495.* This reading is from Chapter 3 of *Black Elk Speaks,* 1932.

615   THE WORK OF CHRISTMAS
Howard Thurman. *See No. 498.*

616   FOR SO THE CHILDREN COME
Sophia Lyon Fahs. *See No. 439.*

617   AND IT CAME TO PASS
Luke 2:1, 4-7. From the *King James Version of the Bible.*

618   IN THIS NIGHT
Dorothee Sölle (1929-) is a German educator and theologian who taught religion in German high schools and German literature at the universities of Cologne and Mainz. Sölle and her husband founded Political Evening Prayer, an ecumenical group for theological reflection and action. She is the author of many books of theology and poetry. This poem comes from *Revolutionary Patience,* 1977.

619   MAGNIFICAT
Weldon Frederick Wooden. *See No. 3.* This reading is an adaptation of Luke 1:46-55, in which Mary, the mother of Jesus, praises God.

620   TO JESUS ON HIS BIRTHDAY
Edna St. Vincent Millay. *See No. 3.* This reading is taken from *Second April [and] The Buck in the Snow,* 1950.

621   WHY NOT A STAR
Margaret Gooding (1922-) is a retired minister of religious education who served congregations in Phoenix, Arizona, and Ottawa, Ontario, and taught at Meadville/Lombard Theological School. In 1985 she received the Unitarian Universalist Association's Angus H. MacLean Award for excellence

in religious education. Her publications include *A Growing-Up Year*, 1988, and *A Stepping-Stone Year*, 1989. This poem was inspired by Sophia Lyon Fahs's poem, "Each night a child is born is a holy night."

622   GOOD FRIDAY
Mark 15:22-25, 29, 32-34, 37. From the *New Revised Standard Version Bible*, 1989. This text has been abridged.

623   EASTER MORNING
Mark 16:2-6, 8.

624   HOPE AGAIN
Clarke Dewey Wells (1930-), a retired Unitarian Universalist minister, has served congregations in Cincinnati, Ohio; Portland, Oregon; South Weymouth, Massachusetts; Lakeland, Florida, and many others. He is the author of several books, including *Sunshine and Rain at Once*, 1981.

625   AN EYE FOR MIRACLES
Diego Valeri (1887-1976) was an Italian classical lyricist whose poetry describes the environment and atmosphere of Venice and the society and culture of Padua, the two cities near his town of birth. His later works concentrate on nature and humankind in love, melancholy, anguish, and struggle. This reading is from *My Name on the Wind: Selected Poems of Diego Valeri*, 1989.

626   LIFE AGAIN
John Banister Tabb. *See No. 335.* This poem is entitled "Evolution."

627   SEASONS OF THE SELF
Max A. Coots. *See No. 489.*

628   ROLLING AWAY THE STONE
Sara Moores Campbell (1943-), a Unitarian Universalist minister, served congregations in Southold, New York, and Rockville, Maryland, before becoming minister of the Unitarian Society of Santa Barbara, California. She is the author of *Into the Wilderness*, the Unitarian Universalist Association's 1990 Meditation Manual.

629   HANUKKAH LIGHTS
Congregation Beth El, Sudbury, Massachusetts.

630 THE FEAST OF LIGHTS
Emma Lazarus (1849-1887), born in New York, New York, was a Jewish poet, essayist, and philanthropist. She is famous for her poem "The New Colossus," which is inscribed on the Statue of Liberty.

631 PASSOVER
Congregation Beth El, Sudbury, Massachusetts.

632 PASSOVER REMEMBERED
Alla Renée Bozarth (1947-) was ordained an Episcopal priest in 1974, one of the first eleven women to do so. She is the author of numerous books of poems as well as works on religion and healing. This reading is taken from *Womanpriest: A Personal Odyssey*, 1978, Bozarth's memoir of her ordination.

633 ATONEMENT DAY
Chaim Stern (1930-) is a rabbi, liturgist, editor, and poet. Stern has written and edited numerous prayerbooks for Reform congregations, including *Gates of Understanding*, 1984; *Gates of Repentance*, edited with Rabbi John D. Rayner, 1979; and *Gates of Prayer*, 1992-93, a series of gender-inclusive prayerbooks. He is the senior rabbi at Temple Beth El in Chappequa, New York. This reading appears in *Gates of Repentance*.

634 ON TURNING
Jack Riemer (1929-) is a Conservative rabbi who serves Temple Beth David in Miami, Florida. He is the editor of several anthologies, including *In the Beginning God: Prayers and Readings for the Days of Awe*, 1969, and *Wrestling with the Angel: Jewish Insights on Death and Mourning*, 1995.

635 A NEW HEART
Chaim Stern. *See No. 633.*

636 BLESS US WITH PEACE
From *Gates of Repentance*, edited by Chaim Stern and John D. Rayner, 1977. *See No. 633.*

637 A LITANY OF ATONEMENT
Robert Eller-Isaacs (1951-) is a Unitarian Universalist minister, poet, and philosopher. Co-minister of the First Unitarian Church of Oakland, California, with his wife, Janne Eller-Isaacs, he previously served the Unitarian Society in Whittier, California.

638   LOVE
I Corinthians 13:1-13. From the *New Revised Standard Version Bible*, 1989.

639   LOVE ONE ANOTHER
I John 4:7-8, 12, 16, 18, 20. From the *New Revised Standard Version Bible*, 1989.

640   THE BEATITUDES
This reading is a composite of Matthew 5:3-9, 13-15, and Luke 6:20-25.

641   THE HEART OF THE TORAH
Leviticus 19:2, 9-16.

642   PSALM 23
Psalm 23, translated by Congregation Beth El, Sudbury, Massachusetts.

643   SHOUT FOR JOY
Psalm 65:8-13.

644   AN UNFAILING TREASURE
Wisdom of Solomon 7:7-14. This reading is from the *New Revised Standard Version Bible*, 1989.

645   SONG OF THE OPEN ROAD
Walt Whitman (1819-1892) was a visionary poet and journalist. His poems, which celebrated democracy, the city, and the human body, were published in *Leaves of Grass*, a collection evolving through nine editions between 1855 and 1892. This reading is from "Song of the Open Road." For Whitman's "allons," here are substituted "together," "forward," and "onward," as in *We Sing of Life*, 1955.

646   THE LARGER CIRCLE
Wendell Berry. *See No. 342*. This text is from "Healing" in *What Are People For?*, 1990.

647   AN ETERNAL VERITY
W. Waldemar W. Argow (1891-1961), an author and poet, served Baptist churches before becoming a Unitarian minister. He served Unitarian congregations in Iowa, New York, and Maryland, and wrote *Beyond*, 1931, a collection of prose poems, and *Victorious Living*, the American Unitarian

Association's 1941 Lenten Manual. This reading is from *We Speak of Life*, 1955.

648   BEGINNERS
Denise Levertov. *See No. 479.* "Beginners" is reprinted in its entirety from *Candles in Babylon*, 1982.

649   FROM GENERATION TO GENERATION
Antoine de St. Exupéry (1900-1944), author of *The Little Prince*, was a French aviator and writer. Disabled as a result of a flying accident, he nevertheless served as a reconnaissance pilot during World War II. After the fall of France, he joined the Air Force in North Africa, where he was shot down and killed in 1944. He is also the author of *The Wisdom of the Sands*, published posthumously in 1950, from which this reading comes.

650   Cherish your doubts
Robert T. Weston. *See No. 369.*

651   THE BODY IS HUMANKIND
Norman Cousins (1912-1990), American essayist, was the editor of the *Saturday Review* for thirty years. He was the author of numerous books on current affairs and on illness and healing; they include *Modern Man Is Obsolete*, 1945, and *Anatomy of an Illness as Perceived by the Patient*, 1979. This healing meditation is from *Human Options: An Autobiographical Notebook*, 1981.

652   THE GREAT END IN RELIGIOUS INSTRUCTION
William Ellery Channing. *See No. 592.*

653   REFLECTIONS ON THE RESURGENCE OF JOY
Dori Jeanine Somers (1931-) is a minister, not in fellowship with the Unitarian Universalist Association, who served the Unitarian Universalist Society of Whittier, California. This poem was a 1973 Christmas gift to the Bangor Unitarian Church, meant to comfort them during an energy crisis with the assurance that joy returns. This text is included in her book *Weeds! Or Wildflowers!*, 1987.

654   IMPASSIONED CLAY
Ralph N. Helverson (1912-) is a retired Unitarian Universalist minister who served churches in Florida, Massachusetts, and New York for nearly

fifty years. This text was written as part of the Unitarian Universalist Association's 1964 Lenten Manual, *Impassioned Clay*.

655   CHANGE ALONE IS UNCHANGING
Heraklietos of Ephesos (Heraclitus of Ephesus) (ca. 480 BCE) was an enigmatic Greek philosopher concerned with the changing nature of the world and with humans' attempts to order it through reason. His work survives only in fragments.

656   A HARVEST OF GRATITUDE
Percival Chubb. *See No. 248.*

657   IT MATTERS WHAT WE BELIEVE
Sophia Lyon Fahs. *See No. 439.*

658   TO RISK
Anonymous.

659   FOR YOU
Walt Whitman. *See No. 645.* This text was arranged and adapted from "Carol of Occupations" by Jacob Trapp. *See No. 139.*

660   TO LIVE DELIBERATELY
Henry David Thoreau (1817-1862), US essayist and poet, wrote, "I was born in the most favored spot on earth—and just in the nick of time, too." The spot was Concord, Massachusetts, where he lived and worked as a caretaker for his friend and neighbor, Ralph Waldo Emerson. *See No. 44.* His vocation was writing, and he produced many books, including *Walden*, 1854, from which this reading comes; *A Week on the Concord and Merrimack Rivers*, 1849; as well as the influential essay, "Civil Disobedience," 1849.

661   THE HEART KNOWETH
Ralph Waldo Emerson. *See No. 44.*

662   STRANGE AND FOOLISH WALLS
A. Powell Davies (1902-1957), born in Birkenhead, England, began his theological service as a Methodist minister in London. In 1928 Davies moved to the United States to a Methodist church in Portland, Maine, where his friendship with the Reverend Vincent B. Silliman (*see No. 42*) led to an interest in Unitarianism. As the minister of the nondenominational Com-

munity Church of Summit, New Jersey, Davies brought his congregation into membership with the American Unitarian Association. In 1944 he was called to All Souls Church in Washington, DC, where he served until his death. In 1958 he received the American Unitarian Association's Award for Distinguished Service to the Cause of Unitarian Universalism. His many books include *American Destiny*, 1942; *America's Real Religion*, 1949; and *The Meaning of the Dead Sea Scrolls*, 1956.

663   ONE SMALL FACE
Margaret Starkey.

664   GIVE US THE SPIRIT OF THE CHILD
Sara Moores Campbell. *See No. 628.*

665   TRANSCENDENTAL ETUDE
Adrienne Rich. *See No. 463.* "Transcendental Etude," from which this excerpt comes, was published in *The Dream of a Common Language*, 1978.

666   THE LEGACY OF CARING
Thandeka (born Sue Booker) (1946-), daughter of a liberal Baptist minister, is an African American ethicist and Unitarian Universalist community minister. A former "Sesame Street" writer and producer, she won an Emmy for her program "As Adam Early in the Morning." She is the author of *The Courage to Feel: Religion and White Middle-Class Poverty in America* and other books, and has taught at San Francisco State University, Williams College, and Union Theological Seminary. Archbishop Desmond Tutu (*see No. 593*) bestowed on her the name "Thandeka," meaning "one who is loved by God."

667   THE CRY OF THE REALIST
Ecclesiastes 1:2-9, 9:7, 11:7-8. This text is found in the *New Revised Standard Version Bible*, 1989.

668   FAITH CANNOT SAVE
James 2:14-18. From the *New Revised Standard Version Bible*, 1989.

669   PSALM 1
Stephen Mitchell (1943-) is a Buddhist-American poet and translator. His translations and adaptations include *The Selected Poetry of Rainer Maria Rilke*, 1982; *Tao Te Ching*, 1988; and *The Gospel According to Jesus*, 1991.

He is also the editor of several anthologies, including *The Enlightened Heart*, 1989, in which this adaptation of Psalm 1 appears.

670   THE WAY
Edwin Muir (1887-1959), Scottish author and critic, first published this poem in *The Labyrinth*, 1949. It appears in his *Collected Poems, 1921-1951*.

671   FREEDOM
John Milton (1608-1674), English poet and pamphleteer, was best known for his epic poem *Paradise Lost*, 1667. A posthumous work, *De Doctrina Christiana*, showed him to be an anti-Trinitarian. This passage from *Areopagitica*, 1644, appeared as arranged in *We Speak of Life*, 1955.

672   Anne Sexton wrote
Judith Meyer (1948-) is a Unitarian Universalist minister serving the Unitarian Community Church of Santa Monica, California. She previously served congregations in New Jersey and New Hampshire; as the director of ministerial education for the Unitarian Universalist Association; and as the UUA's vice president for program. The poem fragment in this reading is from *The Awful Rowing Toward God* by Anne Sexton, 1975.

673   Freely have we received of gifts
Arthur Foote II (1911-), a retired Unitarian Universalist minister, was chair of the commission that compiled *Hymns for the Celebration of Life*, 1964. He served congregations in Stockton and Sacramento, California, as well as Unity Church in St. Paul, Minnesota, where he is minister emeritus. His father, Henry Wilder Foote (1875-1964), was an editor of *The New Hymn and Tune Book*, 1914, and *Hymns of the Spirit*, 1937. His grandfather, Henry Wilder Foote (1838-1889), edited *Hymns of the Church Universal*, 1893, which was completed by his sister, Mary Wilder Tileston, and his brother, Arthur Foote.

674   Let there be an offering to sustain
Brandoch L. Lovely (1928-), a Unitarian Universalist minister, is minister emeritus of the Neighborhood Church in Pasadena, California. He has also served churches in Hingham, Massachusetts, and Austin, Texas.

675   The offering is a sacrament
Ellen Johnson-Fay (1941-), one of the compilers of *Singing the Living Tradition*, is a Unitarian Universalist minister. She is minister of All Souls

Church in New London, Connecticut, having previously served churches in Bethesda, Maryland, and Madison, Connecticut. This reading explains the role of the offering in the Unitarian Universalist liturgy and invites generosity and appreciation in support of liberal religion.

676 So when you are offering your gift
Matthew 5:23-24. These offertory words are from the *New Revised Standard Version Bible*, 1989.

677 The peace which passeth understanding
Drawn from John 14:27 and Philippians 4:7, these closing words are based on the communion benediction in the Anglican *Booke of the Common Prayer*, 1549. They continue to be widely used in Protestant churches.

678 The courage of the early morning's dawning
Anonymous.

679 Be ye lamps unto yourselves
Attributed to Gautama Buddha. *See No. 184.*

680 Because of those who came before, we are
Barbara J. Pescan. *See No. 417.*

681 Deep peace of the running wave to you
Adapted from Gaelic runes.

682 Beauty is before me
From the Navajo of North America, one of the largest, wealthiest, and most progressive Native American tribes. The Navajo reservation covers sixteen million acres including parts of Arizona, New Mexico, and Utah. They call themselves "Dine," meaning "the people." US Army persecution and imprisonment reduced their numbers to fewer than 10,000 by the end of the eighteenth century, but their population has since recovered to more than 125,000.

683 Be ours a religion which, like sunshine, goes everywhere
Theodore Parker (1810-1860), grandson of Captain John Parker of the battle of Lexington, was a great Unitarian preacher. From 1846 to 1860 he was minister of the Twenty-eighth Congregational Society, Boston. Inspired by Transcendentalism and deeply mystical, he was considered heretical by most of his colleagues; nevertheless, he was widely popular. A social radi-

cal and ardent abolitionist, he wrote and published numerous treatises and a few poems. His 1841 sermon on "The Transient and the Permanent in Christianity" argued for a Christianity based not on authority but on the "self-authenticating" teachings of Jesus, a view prevalent later among Unitarians and Universalists.

684   The blessing of truth be upon us
Duke T. Gray (1938-) is a Unitarian Universalist minister who has served congregations in New York, Ontario, Illinois, and Maine. He is the minister of the First Parish Unitarian Church in Malden, Massachusetts. This benediction was written to convey the classic Trinitarian spirituality of God to those whose tradition prevents the usage of the language of II Corinthians 13:13-14.

685   What we call a beginning is often the end
T. S. (Thomas Stearns) Eliot (1888-1965) was an acclaimed poet and playwright who won the 1948 Nobel Prize for Literature. Born in St. Louis, Missouri, Eliot moved to England in 1914 and became a naturalized British subject. He taught French, Latin, mathematics, drawing, geography, and history in a London grammar school and poetry and literature at Cambridge and Harvard universities. His major books of poetry include *Prufrock and Other Observations*, 1917; *The Waste Land*, 1922; and *The Four Quartets*, 1943, from which these words are taken.

686   Go in peace
Mark Belletini. *See No. 73.*

687   Go your ways
John Winthrop Brigham (1914-), a retired Unitarian Universalist minister, served Unitarian and Unitarian Universalist churches for more than forty years. He is the former director of the Unitarian Universalist Service Committee Workcamp in Concord, Massachusetts, and former associate director of the Department of Ministry of the Unitarian Universalist Association. This reading was composed for a ministers' institute in 1959.

688   Hold on to what is good
Nancy Wood. *See No. 481.* These closing words are from *Many Winters*, 1974.

689   Sorrow will one day turn to joy
Paul Robeson. *See No. 462.* These words are from *The Whole World in His Hands: A Pictorial Biography of Paul Robeson* by Susan Robeson, 1981.

690   You shall know the truth
John 8:32. From *The New English Bible*, 1976.

691   Help us to be the always hopeful
May Sarton. *See No. 428.* From *A Grain of Mustard Seed*, 1971.

692   If, here, you have found freedom
Lauralyn Bellamy (1947-), a Unitarian Universalist minister, was ordained at Eno River Unitarian Universalist Fellowship, Durham, North Carolina. She is the organizing minister of the Unitarian Universalist Metro Atlanta North Congregation in Roswell, Georgia.

693   And now, may we have faith in life
Valtyr Emil Gudmundson (1924-1982), born in Lundar, Manitoba, was the district executive for the UUA's Prairie Star District from 1965 until his death. He served Unitarian churches in Maine, Connecticut, Texas, and Minnesota.

694   May the love which overcomes all differences
Frederick E. Gillis. *See No. 501.*

695   Lead me from death to life
Project Ploughshares.

696   To live in this world
Mary Oliver. *See No. 490.* These are the concluding lines of "In Blackwater Woods," from *American Primitive*, 1983.

697   The love and the work of friends and lovers
Wendell Berry. *See No. 342.* This reading comes from "Healing" in *What Are People For?*, 1990.

698   Take courage friends
Wayne B. Arnason (1950-) a Unitarian Universalist minister, serves the Thomas Jefferson Memorial Church in Charlottesville, Virginia. He has also served the Starr King Unitarian Church in Hayward, California, and on the Unitarian Universalist Association staff as a youth programs spe-

cialist. In 1990 he received the UUA's Angus H. MacLean Award for excellence in religious education. This benediction was written and offered at a service about service to others as the primary source of meaning in life.

699   Whatsoever things are true
Philippians 4:8. From the *King James Version of the Bible.*

700   For all who see God, may God go with you
Robert Mabry Doss (1927-), a retired Unitarian Universalist minister, served the First Unitarian Society in Wilmington, Delaware, for more than thirty years. Before his settlement there, he served the Unitarian Church in Rockland, Maryland.

701   We receive fragments of holiness
Sara Moores Campbell. *See No. 628.*

702   Where hate rules, let us bring love
Attributed to St. Francis of Assisi. *See No. 203.*

703   Spirit of the East, be with us always
Anonymous.

704   Go out into the highways and by-ways
John Murray (1741-1815), raised a devout Methodist, was converted to Universalism in Europe by the British preacher James Relly. Ostracized by his family and friends, he immigrated to America, where he organized the First Universalist Church in Gloucester, Massachusetts.

705   If we agree in love
Hosea Ballou (1771-1852), a great figure of American Universalism, was born in Richmond, New Hampshire, the son of a Baptist minister. Influenced by the deism of Ethan Allen, he became a Universalist and was ordained informally in 1794. He founded and edited the *Universalist Magazine*, later *The Trumpet*, and the *Universalist Exposition*. After pastorates in Portsmouth, New Hampshire, and Salem, Massachusetts, he served the Second Society of Universalists of Boston from 1817 until his death. His influential *A Treatise on Atonement*, 1805, taught the invincible love of God and expressed a Unitarian view of Jesus that soon prevailed among Universalists. This text is from the concluding section of *A Treatise on Atonement*.

706   May the light around us guide our footsteps
Kathleen McTigue. *See No. 435.*

707   It is written in the Torah
Deuteronomy 30:19. This text, from the *New Revised Standard Version Bible*, 1989, has been slightly abridged.

708   For you shall go out in joy, and be led back in peace
Isaiah 55:12. In this text, the Second Isaiah (ca. 538 BCE) portrays to his fellow exiles in Babylon the glory of the nation that shall be. These closing words are as found in the *New Revised Standard Version Bible*, 1989.

709   Be doers of the word, and not merely hearers
James 1:22, 25. From the *New Revised Standard Version Bible*, 1989.

710   I lift my eyes to the mountains
Psalm 121:1-2, 7-8. From *The Holy Bible*, translated by James Moffat, 1935.

711   May the eternal bless you and protect you
Numbers 6:24-26. From *The Holy Bible*, translated by James Moffat, 1935.

712   Do not be conformed to this world
Romans 12:2. From the *New Revised Standard Version Bible*, 1989.

713   Keep alert, stand firm in your faith
1 Corinthians 16:13-14. From the *New Revised Standard Version Bible*, 1989.

714   CONGREGATIONAL BLESSING FOR CHILD DEDICATION
Robert Eller-Isaacs. *See No. 637.*

715   YOUR CHILDREN
Kahlil Gibran (1883-1931) was a poet, who wrote in Arabic and English, and painter. Born in Lebanon, he moved to Boston in 1895, attended college in Beirut, studied painting in Paris, and died in New York City. He was the author of *The Prophet*, published in English in 1923, from which this reading is arranged.

716   Hail the day on which a child was born
The Masai people (Plains Niolt people) are nomadic, pastoral people of East Africa. Masai is a linguistic term and includes people who live on the

border of Kenya and Tanzania. One of the most widely studied African people, the Masai are dreaded warriors, fierce hunters, and resistant to change. They are an egalitarian society—one of the few never to have owned slaves. This dedication is from *The Masai, Herders of East Africa* by Sonia Bleeker, 1963.

717   NEW LIFE COMES TO US
George Kimmich Beach. *See No. 332.* This reading was written as a meditation for a child dedication ceremony at the Unitarian Church of Arlington.

718   ALL SOULS
May Sarton. *See No. 428.* This reading is an excerpt from "All Souls," published in *Selected Poems of May Sarton*, 1978.

719   THOSE WHO LIVE AGAIN
George Eliot (Mary Ann Evans) (1819-1880) was a Victorian novelist who pioneered the psychological insight characteristic of modern fiction. Before beginning to write fiction, she served as editor of *The Westminster Review* and a translator of books of religion and philosophy. Her major works include *Adam Bede*, 1859; *Middlemarch*, 1871-1872; and *Daniel Deronda*, 1876.

720   WE REMEMBER THEM
Roland B. Gittelsohn (1910-) is a rabbi and Jewish leader. He has served congregations in New York and Boston and as president of the Central Conference of American Rabbis and other organizations. His books include *The Modern Meaning of Judaism*, 1978, and *Love in Your Life: A Jewish View of Teenage Sexuality*, 1991. This memorial reading is from the 1975 edition of *Gates of Repentence*.

721   THEY ARE WITH US STILL
Kathleen McTigue. *See No. 435.*

722   I THINK CONTINUALLY OF THOSE
Stephen Spender (1909-) is an English poet and literary critic, a contemporary of W. H. Auden (*see No. 334*) and Christopher Isherwood (*see No. 611*). His works of criticism include *The Destructive Element*, 1935, and *The Creative Element*, 1953. This reading comes from his *Selected Poems*, 1934.

723   FLOWER COMMUNION PRAYER
Norbert F. Čapek. *See No. 8.* This text has been revised.

724   CONSECRATION OF THE FLOWERS
Norbert F. Čapek. *See No. 8.*

725   THE SIMPLEST OF SACRAMENTS
Jacob Trapp. *See No. 139.*

726   FOOD FOR THE SPIRIT
Robert Eller-Isaacs. *See No. 637.* The first three stanzas of this reading are based on Jesus' words in Matthew 25:35-36.

727   THE BREAD WE SHARE
Rudolph Nemser (1928-) is a Unitarian Universalist minister serving the Unitarian Church in Cherry Hill, New Jersey. He previously served congregations in Massachusetts, Virginia, and New York.

728   BLESSED ARE THOSE
Adapted by John Buehrens (1947-), sixth president of the Unitarian Universalist Association beginning in 1993. He previously served congregations in Knoxville, Tennessee; Dallas, Texas; and New York, New York. This reading for New Member Recognition services was first included as "Beatitudes for Church Members" in *Our Chosen Faith: An Introduction to Unitarian Universalism*, 1990, written with Forrest Church. The original source(s) of this text is unknown.

729   THE WINDS OF SUMMER
Patricia Shuttee (1925-), writer and community volunteer, was born in Cleveland, Ohio. She wrote children's stories and poetry for family Sundays in Cleveland and readings for adult services at the Unitarian Society of New Haven, Connecticut. This reading was written for a Sunday service.

730   MAKE NOT A BOND OF LOVE
Kahlil Gibran. *See No. 715.* This reading comes from *The Prophet*, 1923.

731   Entreat me not to leave you
Ruth 1:16. From *The Holy Bible*, translated by James Moffat, 1935.

732 FOR MARTIN LUTHER KING, JR.

Toni Vincent (1935-), a Unitarian Universalist minister, was born in New York, New York. She overcame childhood polio and graduated from the University of Southern California with a degree in occupational therapy. After working for ten years as executive director of the Berkeley Community Young Woman's Christian Association, she received her masters of divinity from Starr King Theological Seminary. In 1991 she founded the New Community Congregation in San Francisco, California.

733 A PLACE OF MEETING

Eileen B. Karpeles (1925-), after teaching English for many years, became a Unitarian Universalist minister. Specializing in interim ministry, she has served congregations in six states. This text was written for the 1979 dedication of the Unitarian Universalist Society East Meetinghouse in Manchester, Connecticut.

Pronunciation Guide

Here are pronunciations for seventeen hymns and songs in languages other than English.

171   **N'kosi Sikelel' i Afrika**
A = ah
E = long e
I = ee
O = long o
U = oo
nko = nnkoh (nn is nasal, hit quickly)
ph = P
th = soft T
cha is pronounced as a mixture of sha and cha
cwe pronounced with tongue "click" as in "tisk, tisk, tisk."

172   **Siph' Amandla**
A = ah
E = long e
I = ee
O = long o
U = oo
nko = nnkoh (nn is nasal, hit quickly)
Siph' = seef

176   **Daya Kar Daan Bhakti Ka**
Refrain: Day-yah keh-rah don bok-tee kah,
hah-may pah-rah-mot-mah day-nah.
Day-yah keh-rah hah-mah-ree
Ought-mah may should-dah tah day-nah.

1. Hah-mah-ray dye ah may ah-oh,
prah-boo on koh-may bah-seh jah-oh,
on-day-ray dill may ah cur-ah kay,
pah rah-ma jo-tee jeh-gah day-nah.

2. Bah-hah-day prey-mah-key gun-gah,
dill-oh-men prey-mah-kay saw-gur,

hah-me ah-pus may mill-jul-ker,
prah-boo reh-na see-kah day-nah.

3. Hah-mah-rah dar-mah hoe say-vah.
Ha-ma-rah karma ho see-vah,
sah-dah ee-mon hoh-say-vah,
vah say-vek chur bah-nah day-nah.

177	**Sakura**

Sah-koo-rah
A = ah
I = éé
O = o
U = oo
G is a hard "g" sound
N is a syllable

178   **Raghupati**
Rah-goo-pah-tee Rag-ofv Rah-jah rom
Pah-tee-ta pah-bahn see-tah rom
Eesch-were teh-ray sub-ko sun-mah-tee dee pohg-wahn

180   **Alhamdulillah**
Ahl-hahm-doo-lee-lah

214   **Shabbat Shalom**
Shah-baht shah-loam

216   **Hashiveinu**
Hah-shee-vay-noo, hah-shee-vay-noo
ah-doe-nigh aye-leh-khah
veh-nah-shoo-vah
Khah-daysh
Yah-may-noo-keh-keh-dehm

222   **Mi Y' Malel**
Mi ye-ma-leil ge-vu-rot Yis-ra-eil, o-tan mi yim-neh?
Hein be-chol dor ya-kum ha-gi-bor, ge-eil ha-am.
She-ma! Ba-ya-mim ha-heim ba-ze-man ha-zeh,
Ma-ka-bi mo-shi-a u-fo-deh.
U-ve-ya-mei-nu kol am Yis-ra-eil yit-a-cheid, ya-kum le-hi-ga-eil.

260 **Oshana, Shsira Oshana**
Oh-shah-nah shee-rah
Ha nah-vee hah-vahv-shehm Ah-doh-nye.

280 **Haleluhu**
Hah-leh-loo-hoo, hah-leh-loo-hoo beh-tzeel-tzeh-lay shah-mah
Hah-leh-loo-hoo, hah-leh-loo-hoo beh-tzeel-tzeh-lay teh-roo-ah.
Coal ha-neshah-mah teh-hah-layl-yah.
Hah-leh-loo-yah!

390 **Gaudeamus Hodie**
Gaw-deh-aw-moose aw-de-eh

392 **Hineh Mah Tov**
Hee-nay mah tohv oo-mah-nah-yeem.
Sheh veht ah heem gahm yah hahd.

393 **Jubilate Deo**
Yew-bee-lah-teh, Deh-oh

394 **Hava Nashirah**
Hah-vah nah-shee-rah

400 **Shalom Hayavreem**
Shah-loam hah-vah-reem
La-hit-ray-aht

415 **Hevenu Shalom Aleychem**
Heh-veh-noo shah-loam ah-lay-hem

Name Index

Adams, James Luther, 591
Adams, John Coleman, 294
Adams, Sarah Flower, 87, 411
Addison, Joseph, 283
Adler, Felix, 140
Akhmatova, Anna, 336
Albright, William, 43, 158, 310
Alexander, Mrs. C. F., 228
Alexander, James Waddell, 265
Alford, Henry, 68
Allen, Ethan, 705
Ames, Charles Gordon, 472
Anderson, Francis C., Jr., 546
Anderson, T. J., 321
Angebranndt, Betsy Jo, 28, 121, 136, 147, 197, 238, 354
Angelou, Maya, 539
Anodos. *See* Coleridge, Mary
Argow, W. Waldemar W., 647
Arkin, David, 173, 305
Arnason, Wayne B., 698
Arnold, John, 61
Arnold, Matthew, 88
Asoka (emperor of India), 597
Atkinson, Joy, 445
Attaignant, 287
Auden, W. H., 334, 722
Aurangzeb (emperor of India), 599
Bach, Emmon, 117
Bach, Johann Sebastian, 22, 41, 93, 127, 150, 183, 200, 265, 281, 300, 303, 414
Baez, Joan, 313
Bain, James Leith McBeth, 331
Ballou, Adin, 166
Ballou, Hosea, 129, 705
Ballou, Hosea, II, 132
Bard, Roberta, 207
Baring-Gould, Sabine, 46, 114
Barnby, Sir Joseph, 103

Barnes, John S., 555
Barnett, G. S., 274
Bartók, Béla, 332
Bates, Rachel, 165
Baughan, Raymond J., 485
Bax, Arnold, 120
Bax, Clifford, 120
Beach, George Kimmich, 332, 717
Beach, Seth Curtis, 92
Beardsley, Monroe, 90
Beethoven, Ludwig van, 29, 96, 143, 285, 327
Belafonte, Harry, 313
Bell, Alexander Graham, 118
Bellamy, Lauralyn, 692
Belletini, Mark L., 73, 130, 220, 263, 309, 330, 336, 363, 686
Benjamin, Thomas, 2, 14, 63, 105, 124, 288, 323
Bennett, Elizabeth, 291
Bernard of Clairvaux, 265
Berrigan, Daniel, 590
Berry, Wendell, 342, 465, 483, 646, 697
Berthier, Jacques, 364, 385
Bianco da Siena, 271
Biko, Steven Bantu, 95
Billings, William, 261, 263, 279
Binder, Abraham W., 204, 217
Black Elk, 495, 614
Black Elk, Nicholas. *See* Black Elk
Blake, James Vila, 473
Blake, William, 17, 93, 127, 398
Bleeker, Sonia, 716
Blow, John, 281
Bly, Robert, 608
Bock, Fred, 309
Boeke, Richard Frederick, 8, 28
Bohemian Brethren, 187, 287
Bojaxhiu, Agnes Gonxha. *See* Teresa, Mother

Gannett, William Channing, 39, 40, 45, 57, 187, 215, 473
Garfield, James A., 29
Gascoigne, George, 41
Gastorius, Severus, 76, 267, 344
Gauntlett, Henry John, 228
Gerhardt, Paulus, 265
Gibbons, Kendyl L. R., 51, 125
Gibbons, Orlando, 341
Gibran, Kahlil, 715, 730
Gilbert, Davis, 237
Gilbert, Joyce Timmerman, 322
Gilbert, Richard Seward, 322, 442
Gilbert, William, 114
Giles, John Edwin, 6
Gillis, Frederick E., 501, 694
Gittelsohn, Roland B., 720
Goldman, Emma, 559
Gooding, Margaret, 621
Goodwin, Joan, 410, 446
Gorenko, Anna Andreevna. See Akhmatova, Anna
Gottheil, Gustav, 204, 223
Grant, Robert, 285
Graves, Richard, 134
Gray, Duke T., 684
Greeley, Dana McLean, 326
Greeley, Horace, 575
Green, Fred Pratt, 36
Grieg, Edvard, 398
Griffiths, Vernon, 85
Grigolia, Mary E., 396
Grotenhuis, Dale, 79
Gruber, Franz Xavier, 251, 252
Gudmundson, Valtyr Emil, 693
Guttormsson, Guttormur J., 49
Hafiz. See Shams Ud-Dun Mohammad Hafiz
Hale, Edward Everett, 457
Hall, Americk, 94
Ham, Marion Franklin, 13, 145
Hammarskjöld, Dag, 455, 486
Hancock, Eugene Wilson, 112
Handel, George Frederick, 281

Hanson, Heather Lynn, 229
Harlow, Samuel Ralph, 276
Harper, Frances Ellen Watkins, 153
Hart, Connie Campbell, 18
Hartig, Xavier Ludwig, 262
Hartman, Gertrude, 589
Haspl, Bodhana Čapek, 28
Hassler, Hans Leo, 110, 265
Hatton, John, 25, 35
Hatton, John Liptrott, 25
Haydn, Franz Joseph, 81, 190, 283, 285
Haydn, Michael, 285
Heber, Reginald, 26, 39
Hedge, Frederick Henry, 33, 200
Heinlein, Robert, 163
Helmore, Thomas, 225
Helverson, Ralph N., 654
Henllan, John Roberts, 122, 269
Henry VIII (king of England), 88
Heraclitus of Ephesus. See Heraklietos of Ephesos
Heraklietos of Ephesos, 655
Herbert, George, 89
Herman, Nikolaus, 22, 41, 93
Heschel, Abraham J., 497
Hewett, Phillip, 440
Hildegard of Bingen, 27, 493
Hille, Waldemar, 9, 157, 173, 331
Hintze, Jacob, 150
Hirsch, Nurit, 146
Hirschhorn, Linda, 155
Hodges, Edward, 29
Hoffmann, A. H., 42
Holmes, John, 11, 164
Holmes, John Haynes, 82, 474
Holst, Gustav Theodore, 120, 241, 249
Hopkins, John Henry, Jr., 259
Hopson, Hal H., 34, 328
Horder, W. Garrett, 119
Hornbook, Wallace, 70
Hosmer, Frederick Lucian, 45, 53, 96, 105, 114, 269, 270, 272, 473
Housman, A. E., 98
Hovhaness, Alan, 408

Neale, John Mason, 225
Neander, Joachim, 278
Near, Holly, 170
Neihardt, John G., 495
Nelson, Earl, 103
Nemser, Rudolph, 727
Newton, John, 205, 206
N'hat Hanh, Thich, 505, 554
Niebuhr, Reinhold, 461
Niles, Daniel, 353
Noble, T. Tertius, 42
Noyes, Alfred, 339
Nyberg, Anders, 172
Oakeley, Frederick, 253
Odell, George E., 468
Oler, Kim, 163
Oliver, Mary, 490, 536, 696
Oliver, William E., 331
Olivers, Thomas, 215
Oppenheim, James, 109
Owen-Towle, Carolyn S., 492
Owen-Towle, Thomas, 492
Pachelbel, Johann, 386
Page, Nick, 163
Palestrina, Giovanni Pierluigi da, 107
Palfi, Marton, 322
Palmer, Edwin C., 380
Parker, Archbishop, 88
Parker, John, 683
Parker, Theodore, 683
Parks, Rosa, 156
Parry, Charles Hubert Hastings, 17, 337, 359
Parry, John, 269
Parry, Joseph, 174
Patton, Kenneth L., 191, 303, 308, 310, 339, 378, 379, 437, 443, 444
Persichetti, Vincent, 250
Pescan, Barbara J., 417, 506, 534, 680
Petri, Theodoric, 241, 249
Petti, Anthony, 27
Phillips, Larry, 37, 130, 352
Pickett, Helen R., 309, 512
Pickett, O. Eugene, 309, 512

Piercy, Marge, 567, 568, 585
Pierpoint, Folliott Sandford, 21
Pilsbury, Amos, 213
Plenn, Doris, 108
Pliny the Younger, 21
Pohl, David C., 436
Pohl-Kosbau, Leslie, 451
Poley, Joyce, 168
Pomeroy, Vivian Towse, 477
Pope, Alexander, 91, 189
Porter, Philip A., 50, 81, 389
Prabhavananda, Swami, 611
Praetorius, Christoph, 362
Praetorius, Hieronymous, 412
Praetorius, Michael, 393
Price, Charles, 100
Price, Frank W., 353
Prichard, Rowland Hugh, 140, 166, 207
Project Ploughshares, 695
Proulx, Richard, 196
Purcell, Henry, 295
Quaile, Robert N., 1
Quang, Nguyen-Duc, 59, 314
Quimada, Toribio S., 182
Rainey, Ma, 199
Ramabhadran, Sanjeev, 176
Ravel, Maurice, 17
Ravenscroft, Thomas, 185
Ray, James Earl, 584
Rayner, John D., 633, 636
Rebenlein, Georg, 145
Redhead, Richard, 132
Redner, Lewis H., 246
Reeb, James, 30
Reese, Curtis, 40
Reilly, Jim, 286
Relly, James, 704
Reynolds, Malvina, 313
Rice, Joyce Painter, 295
Rich, Adrienne, 463, 665
Richmond, Daniel, 321
Ricker, Roger R., Jr., 3
Rickey, Patrick L., 128, 170, 363, 365

Riemer, Jack, 634
Rinkart, Martin, 32
Ripley, Samuel, 460
Ripley, Sarah Alden, 460
Robb, John Donald, 230
Roberts, Griffith, 140
Robeson, Paul, 368, 462, 689
Robeson, Susan, 689
Robinson, Christine, 448, 454
Robinson, Robert, 126
Robinson, Wayne Bradley, 405
Rodigast, S., 76
Roethke, Theodore Huebner, 54
Roger, Brother, 364
Rogers, Sally, 131
Rossetti, Christina Georgina, 241, 296
Rossetti, Dante Gabriel, 241
Rossetti, Gabriele, 241
Routley, Eric, 410
Rowan, William P., 198
Rowley, Charity, 298
Roy, Rammohun, 474
Rumi, Jalal al-Din Rumi, 188
Ruspini, Louise, 361
Rzepka, Jane, 510
Saadi, 609
Saint Exupéry, Antoine de, 649
Sanders, Robert L., 5, 284, 322
Sandys, William, 237
Santayana, George, 341
Sarton, May, 428, 691, 718
Savage, Minot Judson, 77, 293
Schalk, Carl Flentge, 334
Schein, Johann Hermann, 127, 183, 300, 308
Scherf, Royce J., 232
Schreck, Nancy, 425
Schubert, Franz, 327
Schulz, William F., 429, 459
Schumann, Robert, 327
Schumann, Valentin, 110
Schweitzer, Albert, 447
Scott, Clinton Lee, 438, 565
Scott, Jim, 163, 167, 316, 347

Seaburg, Carl G., 37, 62, 124, 228, 234, 338, 352, 358
Sealth, Noah, 550
Sears, Edmund Hamilton, 244
Seattle, Chief. *See* Sealth, Noah
Secunda, S., 214
Seed, John, 570
Seeger, Pete, 313
Segal, Joseph, 402
Segal, Nathan, 402
Sen, Keshab Chandra, 474
Senesh, Hannah, 450
Senghas, Dorothy Caiger, 349
Senghas, Robert E., 349
Servet, Miguel, 13
Servetus, Michael. *See* Servet, Miguel
Sexton, Anne, 672
Shams od-Din Mohammad Hafez. *See* Shams Ud-Dun Mohammad Hafiz
Shams of Tabriz, 188
Shams Ud-Dun Mohammad Hafiz, 607
Shapiro, Rami M., 503
Shaw, Martin, 226
Shepard, Odell, 161
Shumaker, Ann, 589
Shuttee, Patricia, 729
Sibelius, Jean, 159, 318
Sigismund (king of Sweden), 249
Silliman, Vincent B., 40, 42, 44, 133, 249, 259, 287, 380, 414, 466, 662
Simons, George Francis, 460
Simos, Miriam. *See* Starhawk
Sjolund, Paul, 239
Skrine, John Huntley, 358
Slater, Gordon, 405
Sleeth, Natalie, 390, 413
Slegers, Mark, 280
Smart, Henry, 270
Smit, Leo, 292
Smith, Alfred Morton, 54, 164, 191
Smith, Walter Chalmers, 273
Smith, William Farley, 169, 208
Sölle, Dorothee, 618
Somers, Dori Jeanine, 653

Somerville, Thomas, 232
Sontongo, Enoch Mankayi, 171
Spencer, Herbert, 77
Spender, Stephen, 722
Stainer, John, 237
Stanford, Charles Villiers, 36, 241
Starhawk, 517, 524
Starkey, Margaret, 663
Steele, Anne, 69
Steffy, John W., 79
Stein, Leopold, 223
Stern, Chaim, 450, 468, 633, 635, 636
Stevenson, John A., 47
Stevenson, Robert Louis, 195
Stobaeus, 521
Stone, Lloyd, 159
Storey, John Andrew, 2, 19, 71, 102,
   160, 174, 186, 193, 241, 297, 302,
   307, 320, 350, 353
Sullivan, Arthur Seymour, 114
Symonds, John Addington, 138
Tabb, John B., 335, 626
Tagore, Rabindranath, 185, 191, 197,
   519, 529, 540, 608, 612
Tallis, Thomas, 88, 330
Tans'ur, W., 272
Taylor, Billy, 151
Taylor, Cecily, 134
Taylor, Cyril Vincent, 64, 77, 90, 339
Tchaikovsky, Piotr Ilyich, 327
Teasdale, Sara, 329
Tegh Bahadur, 599
Teilhard de Chardin, Pierre, 549
Tennyson, Alfred, 58, 143
Teresa, Mother, 562
Thakura, Ravindranatha. *See*
   Rabindranath Tagore
Thandeka, 666
Thelander, Albert Hill, 449
Thoreau, Henry David, 161, 660
Thorn, Emily L., 112
Thurman, Howard, 498, 615
Tileston, Mary Wilder, 673
Tisserand, Jean, 296

Torrence, Ridgely, 284
Trajan (emperor of Rome), 21
Trapp, Jacob, 139, 148, 441, 482, 659,
   725
Trench, Richard Chenevix, 299
Troeger, Thomas H., 158
Truth, Sojourner, 201
Tubman, Harriet, 104, 210
Tutu, Desmond Mpilo, 172, 401, 593,
   666
Ulp, Grace, 78
Ungar, Lynn Adair, 188
Untermeyer, Louis, 1, 85
Uvanuk, Shaman, 526
Valeri, Diego, 625
Valerius, Adrian, 67
Van Dyke, Henry, 29
Vaughan Williams, Ralph, 7, 17, 49,
   52, 57, 65, 89, 103, 106, 165, 203,
   209, 224, 240, 247, 271, 289, 324,
   326, 338, 341
Victoria (queen of England), 282
Vincent, Toni, 732
Vogt, Von Ogden, 476
von Brachel, Peter, 203
von Schiller, Friedrich, 327
Vulpius, Melchior, 175
Wade, John Francis, 253
Waggoner, A., 76, 344
Walden, Mary Allen, 116, 151, 162,
   201, 210, 407
Walker, Alice, 564
Walker, George Theophilus, 60
Walker, William, 15, 18, 44, 66, 161,
   193, 232, 312, 313, 315, 411
Walsh, Walter, 44
Walton, Isaak, 135
Watts, Isaac, 245, 281, 381, 382
Weaver, John, 225, 410
Webb, Charles H., 70, 299, 313
Webb, George James, 144
Wells, Barbara, 431
Wells, Clarke Dewey, 624
Wesley, Charles, 83, 268

Wesley, John, 268
Wesley, Samuel Sebastian, 83
Wesley family, 205
Weston, Robert Terry, 369, 530, 538, 547, 650
Westwood, Horace, 403
Wetzel, Richard D., 263
Whalum, Wendell, 141, 348
Wheatley, Phillis, 97
Wheeler, Gerald, 325
Whitefield, George, 205
Whitman, Walt, 356, 645, 659
Whittier, John Greenleaf, 9, 10, 70, 75, 122, 274
Wile, Frances Whitmarsh, 57
Williams, Charles, 493
Williams, L. Griswold, 471
Williams, Robert, 269
Williams, Theodore Chickering, 242
Williams, Thomas, 12, 138
Williams, Thomas John, 119
Williams, Velma C., 242
Willis, Richard Storrs, 244
Wilson, Edwin Henry, 113
Wilson, John, 272
Winkley, Lala, 514
Winkworth, Catherine, 32, 278
Winter, Paul, 163, 167
Wittwe, Georg, 145
Wolfe, Thomas, 555
Wolff, William, 177
Wood, Nancy, 481, 552, 553, 688
Wooden, Enoch, 306
Wooden, Samuel Daley, 31
Wooden, Weldon Frederick, 3, 31, 96, 306, 340, 619
Wordsworth, William, 25, 333, 499
Worgan, John, 61
Wotton, Henry, 135
Wren, Brian, 23, 31, 198, 275, 317, 325, 408, 412
Wright, Samuel Anthony, 318
Wright, Frank Lloyd, 308
Wyatt, Janet, 337

Wyeth, John, 53, 126
Wylder, Betty A., 109, 131, 221, 305, 311, 361
Wyton, Alec, 4
Yarrow, Peter, 221
Young, Carlton R., 18, 20, 23, 98, 243, 275, 401
Young, Michael G., 91
Zangwill, Israel, 418
Zanotti, Barbara, 121
Zeller, 21
Zimmermann, Heinz Werner, 84